THE
INNER
CHILD

Understanding Your Child's Emotional Growth in the First Six Years of Life

Dr. H. Paul Gabriel & Robert Wool

BALLANTINE BOOKS • NEW YORK

Copyright © 1990 by H. Paul Gabriel and Premier Cru Books, Inc.

All rights reserved under International and Pan-American Copyright Conventions. Published in the United States of America by Ballantine Books, a division of Random House, Inc., New York, and simultaneously in Canada by Random House of Canada Limited, Toronto.

Library of Congress Catalog Card Number: 89-49560

ISBN 0-345-36280-2

This edition published by arrangement with Times Books, a division of Random House, Inc.

Manufactured in the United States of America

First Ballantine Books Edition: July 1992

Cover photo by Elizabeth Hathon

"Dr. Gabriel, a seasoned child psychiatrist, with the help of Robert Wool, has presented a practical, down-to-earth guide for parents. He describes how parents' expectations—often unrealistic—can interfere with the real parent-child relationship. The authors discuss differences in children's inborn temperament, the mother-child fit, bonding in fathers, differences between mothers and fathers, parenting style. Good common sense pervades this book. The authors offer suggestions for setting down patterns to last a lifetime, such as reading together before bedtime, listening respectfully and attentively to others, and answering questions with honesty. Numerous vignettes are presented from Dr. Gabriel's practice, such as preparing children for surgery and discussions about divorce or death of a loved one.

"I am planning to recommend it to dozens of parents and pre-school teachers. It is a serious exposition of the childhood developmental stages, yet it is written in a lucid fashion without jargon so that individuals without psychological training can understand their young children's behavior and use effective strategies in coping with them."

CLARICE J. KESTENBAUM, M.D.
Clinical Professor of Psychiatry
Division of Child Psychiatry
College of Physicians & Surgeons
of Columbia University

CONTENTS

INTRODUCTION

In a general way, I knew from my own practice of child psychiatry and the questions I heard from anxious mothers and fathers about their infants, that a book like this was needed. "Why is she suddenly throwing her food all over the place?" "Our son is driving us crazy. He won't do anything we ask." "Have we ruined our daughter? Traumatized her?"

The need became clearer when Bob Wool came to me with an idea. Bob is the author of several books and a psychology maven, and most important, at that time he was the father of two infant girls. He and his wife, Bridget, had read everything available but had yet to find "the psychological Spock," as he called it. Where was the book that explained why his daughters were doing what they were doing, that suggested what was going on inside their heads, that guided him and Bridget toward the more enlightened ways of parenting? Where was the book that answered the psychological questions and anxieties that all new parents share, in the way that other books described the causes and treatment of a rash on the buttocks at six months?

Together, we have tried in *The Inner Child* to provide that guide, a book that offers background and perspective along with practical solutions.

While we are specific in our discussion, we do not offer a list of recipes. One of the secrets a child psychiatrist knows is that parents are more effective than they think they are. With sufficient perspective and informed approaches to problems, they are amazingly well equipped to raise children on their own.

Beyond the customary areas of discussion in a book of this kind, we have considered a number of conditions and problems of our society that parents confront today—problems of surrogate parents in homes where both parents work, of divorce, of adoption, of religion in mixed marriages.

Throughout the book, we have tried to make clear that the roots of trouble in children have complex origins. A single incident, often a single lapse of patience on the part of a parent, does not "traumatize" a child. There are genetic, biologic, and environmental strains feeding any serious disorder, and a psychological disturbance occurs only after continuous emotional turmoil in a family.

Finally, we have made the point that consistency on the part of parents, along with structure and discipline, matters to infants—which does not mean that parents must be forbidding, punishing ogres. There are a variety of healthy, supportive ways parents can fuse these qualities into the fabric of a child's life.

This book is written for men and women, for mothers and fathers. Children need both. If one parent comes to me in my practice for help, I insist on meeting with both parents. Still, mothers remain the primary caregivers in the families of our society, and so we have written this book with them in mind as the primary readers. This has required certain stylistic and editorial adaptations, which we hope will not in any way make fathers feel excluded.

Enjoy your children. We hope our book helps.

—Dr. Paul Gabriel

1

The First Joys, the First Anxieties

Our children are the source of untold joy, of new levels of love, as well as of great anxiety.

In the first years of our child's life, when he is so tiny, apparently so frail and helpless, so dependent on us, we worry first about his physical well-being. Actually, he is stronger than he appears to be.

No less meaningful, and perhaps more worrisome, is his psychological well-being. I say more worrisome because in the physical realm there is often a clear problem—a rash on the buttocks—and a prescribed solution—a medicated cream. Psychological and emotional problems, however, are frequently unclear in their origin, and dealing with them is rarely as simple and direct as using a tube of cream from the local drugstore.

Further, there is little or no helpful communication. Your three-year-old can and will come to you and say, "My foot hurts." He will not be able to come to you and say, "I am angry because I feel completely neglected by you and my father and that is why I smacked that kid in the sandbox today."

In practicing psychiatry for more than twenty-five years, I have found parents looking for guidance on two levels. They want to understand and cope with an immediate crisis. "My kid won't do anything I tell him to. He has a tantrum practically anytime I ask him to do anything." "All of a sudden, she's throwing food. She won't eat anything. All she'll do is throw it across the room." "He won't play with other kids, doesn't want anything to do with them. And at home, he wants to dress up in his sister's clothes. He's a boy and he wants to dress up in girls' clothes." These are all troubling developments, and the parents who bring them to me are desperate for immediate solutions.

Then there is the need for broader guidance. Coping with fits, for example, is important, and it allows a family to regain a degree of control and peace in its life. But that does not provide the broader picture and perspective that parents want, that parents need in order to anticipate and comprehend what their children are going through. Some parents have explained it to me as a way of being a step ahead of their children, prepared for them and for the next psychological stage of development. "Every year at the beginning of the school year," one mother said to me, "I want the teacher to tell me, in addition to all the new skills they will be working on, what the new psychological phases will be. 'Here's what to expect this year,' I want them to say. But they never do."

It is clear to me that if parents do have that perspective they probably will be better parents. To begin with, they will be less anxious. When their child's behavior takes a turn, they will be considerably better able to cope. They will be able to interact with their children in ways that are psychologically more healthful for the child and themselves.

A child's psychological growth evolves like a symphony, playing out several rich themes. The daily interplay between parents and child is obviously one major source. But it is not by any means the only source, as many parents think. Indeed, such a misunderstanding puts additional pressure on the parents.

They tend to view themselves as the purveyors of trauma and neuroses.

Much of your child's development is out of your hands. Much of it stems from the child's biology, much from heredity, the luck of the genes. Much is the result of the culture around you.

In this book, I try to encompass all these elements and I urge you to read the whole book. It is important to grasp the full sweep of these years. By all means, use the book as a guide to any specific problems that might arise. But don't just pick at it. You'll be cheating yourself and your child.

Because I think the broad perspective is so important—What can I expect this year?—the first section of each chapter tells you that. It reviews the psychological, biologic, and scientific material I think you'll need as background for each specific phase of your child's psychological life.

Then, in a section called "The Real World," I apply the theoretical background material to everyday problems and situations, the common questions and anxieties and dilemmas that confront parents. Obviously, I do not have all the answers to every problem that might arise, but this section should help you to develop your own methods for solving problems and will provide useful guidance.

At the end of the book there is a chapter called "Special Conditions." Here I discuss aspects of parenting that require an understanding of how cultural influences affect the psychological life of both child and family: religious education, divorce, adoption, raising a super-child, urban life and children, and single-parent families, among others.

I have organized this guide to a child's first six years, with a nod to Erik Erikson, into five stages of development. They are the primary paths of psychological growth during these years.

Stage 1: The Age of Dependency
(birth to 14 months)

This is a time when your infant is almost totally dependent on you, unable because of his lack of motor skills and physical development to do much of anything by himself. For him it is a time of confinement, but during this period of seeming inactivity occur the first stages in the development of the child's personality.

Stage 2: The Age of Exploration
(14 to 30 months)

The infant can finally move about on his own and begins to explore his universe. He starts testing his autonomy and hears an awful lot of "no, no, no" and "don't, don't, don't" from his watchdog parents. Your baby will experiment with his new environment. He will put fingers into electric outlets, crawl into kitchen cabinets, pull on tablecloths. It is also the time Freud labeled "anal," and during this period you and your child will first come into substantial confrontation and conflict.

Stage 3: The Age of Communication
(30 to 48 months)

Your child's curiosity is tremendously heightened. He begins to test reality, to strike out in the world. He is developing skills of communication and is making up stories, fantasies, fears, monsters. Culture begins to make new demands with the start of nursery school. This is also a time of sexual awakening and curiosity: Freud's phallic period and the beginning of the Oedipal period. It is also Piaget's concrete period, Erikson's period of initiative. It is a time of narcissism and of Freud's pleasure principle.

Stage 4: The Age of Separation
(48 to 60 months)

Your child's struggle with growing up begins in earnest, his sexual curiosity increases, and Freud's Oedipal conflict is intense. It is a time of showing off, of saying "Look at me." Your child will begin to do things by himself, and little girls will start dressing up, playing house. It is a period when your child trusts you but also resents you.

Stage 5: The Age of Early Independence
(60 to 72 months)

During this period, your child begins an intense struggle between becoming independent and fearing that independence. He now has enough motor coordination to master numerous tasks, to sit at a table, to draw letters. Cultural influences are strong and the matter of goals and competition with other children enters his and your lives.

Before moving to the next chapter and Stage 1, let me comment on a few matters, questions that frequently arise during pregnancy. The prenatal period is essentially beyond the boundaries of this book, yet how you deal with the questions that loom so large during that time can have a significant psychological effect on your home and family and very much shape the kind of parents you and your husband will be.

WILL I BE ABLE TO TAKE CARE OF MY BABY?
WILL I BE A GOOD PARENT?

I think every potential parent worries about this. What could be more normal? Especially in these days, when most of us grow up in small families without many brothers and sisters in the sort of caregiving roles that were common in the nineteenth century. We have no experience in the simplest mechanics of the job—feeding the baby, bathing her, even diapering her. We have no grasp of the more complicated aspects—what she needs emotionally, for example, to develop in a full and healthy way. And yet, in months this tiny living creature is going to be completely dependent on you.

In fact, it's very healthy to be anxious about your first child. (With your second one, by the way, you'll be so much more relaxed, you'll worry that you're being careless.) It's like being one of the best soldiers in a battle. People—soldiers or new mothers—think better and more clearly when touched by a bit of fear. But there is help out there.

There are books, of course. To suggest a few, you might want to look at Alan Guttmacher's *Pregnancy, Birth and Family Planning*. Also, the standard, *Baby and Child Care*, by Dr. Benjamin Spock and Dr. Michael Rothenberg. Three more focused on psychology are *The Uses of Enchantment*, by Bruno Bettelheim, Selma Fraiberg's *The Magic Years*, and *Your Child as a Person*, by Alex Thomas.

You can rely on your newly found obstetrician, and soon on your pediatrician. And there are other parents. Not necessarily your own parents. You would probably be more comfortable talking with your peers who are parents and have life-styles similar to yours. If you're working and going to be a working mother, reach out to anyone you know who has done it. Talk over your worries, the problems you anticipate, with her. If you are going to be a full-time mother, reach out to your neighbors in the same situation.

There might well be another pregnant woman in your large apartment building, or in your neighborhood, whom you've seen around but never really talked to. Start talking. Many new friendships start over new babies. You can share anxieties now, as well as insights and knowledge. An awful lot of worry can vanish simply when you hear someone else say, "God, I woke up in the middle of the night the other night crazy over the very same thing. . . ."

Finally, every now and then during these months, pause and remember that you are not the only or the first people to have a child with no prior experience or credentials. I would guess there have been several billion before you on this planet alone.

WILL IT DESTROY OUR MARRIAGE?

The truth is that a baby will change a marriage. What you can't anticipate, however, is the degree of change, and both husband and wife have to make substantial adjustments if their marriage is to grow along with their child.

The fact is that raising a child is work. There are continual trade-offs, the deepest pleasures in exchange for some sacrifices and rough times.

Two reasonably mature people have no reason to fear that a baby might destroy their marriage, unless—and this is a major unless—their marriage is shaky to begin with.

Never ever try to save a marriage by having a baby. You will almost certainly ruin the marriage and damage the child. A weak marriage simply cannot stand the strains and stress that come with a baby.

Consider just one aspect: the general care of the child. A baby needs attention, love, stimulation, care. It is hoped especially these days, that those tasks will not be left to the woman alone. But, as I have seen in any number of shaky marriages, men have a way of copping out. They do it without even thinking about it. Often they disappear into their work, hiding behind the standard dodge: "With the baby, I've got to earn more than ever." Their wives quite naturally grow increasingly resentful, and you can imagine how that shreds the already weak ties between them.

All of this is especially true in our contemporary culture, where the tendency is to divorce rather than struggle with a complicated set of human problems.

However, I don't believe in sustaining a marriage only because there is a child. As recently as 1961, when I first started to practice child psychiatry, a more Victorian view prevailed. Even in the worst marriages, people forced themselves to stay together because there were children. But chronically disturbed marriages were the root of many cases of disturbed infants. If you were treating a troubled child and learned that she was from a home with a rocky marriage, you knew the turmoil was part of that child's problems.

SHARING THE PREGNANCY

You think of the baby as the most special thing you and your husband can share—and of the pregnancy as a miraculous experience.

I don't mean to diminish your loving feelings, but in fact, I think you'll find that the sharing has limits. Not that you want to deprive him, but there are some natural elements involved here.

To begin with, you are carrying the baby in your body. That makes a difference. It is always with you. When your husband leaves your company, he leaves the baby—and the preoccupation with the baby—behind.

You will both be astonished when the fetus starts kicking, and there is something only you and he can know in that shared moment when he puts his hand on your belly and feels those movements. But chances are that during the last three months of the pregnancy the magic will dim for him. You will still be amazed and thrilled by this fetal communication, but he will be somewhat blasé.

There are some important differences between women and men, between mothers and fathers, to recognize here, and some are hotly debated. If you can recognize them, nevertheless, I think you will be able to understand extremely important psychological dynamics going on between you and your husband during pregnancy and your first years as parents.

There are biological functions that are unique to females, and having a baby is one of them. That unique phenomenon is a part of the special bonding process that goes on between a mother and her infant. I'm not talking here about the "maternal instinct," or alluding to "woman's role in society," issues that sometimes get wrapped into this discussion. The evidence is that the so-called maternal instinct is hardly provable. It was once an accepted rationalization for limiting the roles and opportunities of women in society. Women had that instinct, went the argument, so their function was to produce and mother babies, period.

I mean instead the knowledge of what it is to bear a child, to know that organism is within you. I believe that it generates a closeness in the early years between mother and baby that fathers have to be taught. Let me add that even though it is no longer very popular to say so, most psychiatrists and child developmentalists really do feel that this special maternal sense of unity exists.

The fetus is a piece of the mother, and she and the baby have a special bond after it is born. That's why, for example, I believe a mother can change her baby's diapers and clean up after her when she gets sick with less discomfort and disgust than a father. The father will do it, but he has to be trained, has to condition himself. Indeed, fathers tell me with mild guilt in their voices that they were surprised at the revulsion they experienced when they first confronted their baby's diaper full of excrement.

All of this is going to affect the way you and your husband relate to the baby, and so to each other. You are going to feel your pregnancy from the beginning, especially when fatigue and morning sickness reach you. Your husband may be accommodating, solicitous, but he is not physically altered. Women have told me that the reality of parenthood didn't start for their husbands until the baby was home. The women had gone through the nine months of pregnancy, but not until they saw the baby every day at home did the fathers really comprehend what had happened. Even then it took some months before the men were engaged in their children.

The father has to learn to be attached, while the mother has been physically attached by an umbilical cord for nine months.

This difference between each parent's relationship with the infant is somewhat magnified by the fact that the baby is not very responsive during its first few months on earth. If your husband doesn't have the experience and the attachment I speak of, and he can't even get a smile from his child, despite his effort in trying to be a good father, some connection is missing. It will come, but until it does, neither you nor he should worry about it or feel guilty about a lack of expected feeling. Women are different from men in profound ways, and this is one of the results.

DIFFERENCES BETWEEN WOMEN AND MEN, MOMMIES AND DADDIES

Times have changed; some things have not. In our culture, the woman is still perceived as the psychological center of the family.

There is an expectancy with most husbands, even ones who change diapers, as well as with society and the greater framework of the family and all people who relate to the family, that the woman is the person with the primary responsibility for running the household. Psychologically, she becomes the most important member of the family.

This is true even for the working mother. She is still expected to be the homemaker, the person who takes care of the child, who makes arrangements, who copes with the housekeeper/baby-sitter (her surrogate), who talks to the butcher and the pediatrician.

To be sure, the husband today is most often an active collaborator, but the woman remains the central figure. It is one of the additional psychological burdens on a working mother. Ten-year-old-boys are still being brought up to turn first to their mothers when there's trouble at home, or when they have a question or need information, guidance, reassurance, first aid, love. And it doesn't matter to them if she works in an office or is in the next room. It's ingrained in our culture, and it will take a long time to unlearn it. Women have had this role for about six million years, and have done it rather well, no matter how hard they worked outside the household.

There are, of course, single-parent homes where the only parent is a man—a divorced father who has custody of his children, a widower, or a man alone who has adopted a child—and where there is no surrogate mother. Those men can assume the central role, but it takes an awful lot of work on their part.

It is very tough for children and father to make that transition. I've had many children brought to me who were in dire circumstances because the absence of a mother was more than they could cope with.

All of this is not to say that there can't be great sharing of roles within a home. Nor does it suggest that if a woman assumes her historic central role she can't have any others. We'll discuss sexual roles and sexual identities and their significant differences further in the book. But let me say now that a woman can be a police officer, a miner, or a terrorist, but she still remains a female on the basis of her biology. Conversely, a man can change hundreds, thousands, of diapers, but his baby will rarely perceive him as the natural fulcrum of the family.

For you and your husband not to understand these realities could lead to confusion, frustrations, and unnecessary tensions between you. It could also permit considerable resentment on your part over the fact that somehow you are shouldering more than your fair share of the work and the responsibility for the child.

2

The Age of
Dependency

(birth to 14 months)

Newborn babies are, despite their fragile appearance, quite resilient. Growing for eight to nine months inside the womb, your infant has been building up defenses to withstand the outside world. Without your doing anything or teaching him anything, he will breathe, he will eat, he will defecate. He will automatically maintain his homeostasis, heart rate, respiratory rate, sleep cycles, and other functions. And he can let his needs be known by yelling.

Ignoring your own postchildbirth exhaustion and what I call postpartum blues, you and your husband may well take up sentry positions, sitting guard over your baby most of the day and night. Every cry will be an alarm, shocking you upright and into action.

Finally, after some two weeks of rather blinding fatigue, your anxiety will begin to level off. You will start to notice that indeed your baby has survived, that even though you hardly possessed experience—as even a baby-sitter, never mind as a mother—you have done what had to be done. There were even times during this siege, you will recall, when you actually slept, and still nothing happened to your infant.

One caution for these rough days and for the months

to come: During this time, it's important to understand
that if your baby cries a lot she is not trying to make
your life miserable, nor is she even aware that her
noisemaking and irritability are affecting you and others
around her. Certainly, she is not trying to manipulate
you and your husband.

While we understand some patterns of development
and growth in this initial period, we don't really know
what is going on inside your baby's head, because the
baby can't communicate with us in a way that gives us
insight.

The signaling between you is very simplistic. Crying
is an infant's main method of communicating, and a
number of things can trigger it—some serious, some
not. By crying, she will tell you she's uncomfortable.
But you won't know if the problem stems from gas gur-
gling around, or because the room is too light or too
dark, or because she is wet or hungry.

This is a very biological period, and what's happening
with your baby is going on automatically and inexorably.

THREE AREAS OF DEVELOPMENT:
BIOLOGICAL, PSYCHOLOGICAL, CULTURAL

Your baby's nursery room will be a great messy lab-
oratory of sorts for the first fourteen months, and you
and your husband will be both observers and active participants. You will watch the startling changes through
which your baby evolves, and also feed him much of
the emotional nourishment and input he requires.

During this time, there are three great areas of development: biological, psychological, and cultural.

As you'll see, there are certain things about the biology of your child that are inexorable; they happen no
matter what you do.

Walking, for example. Your baby starts life quite unable to walk. By the time this period of dependency is
completed (at around fourteen months), most children

will be walking. Even if you wanted to, there's very little you could do to alter that time frame. Some primitive tribes tie babies onto their mothers' backs or swaddle them for twelve months. When they let them go, the children start to walk very soon after. It is programmed into a baby's system.

Or consider communication. At the beginning, as I noted, about all your baby will do to communicate is cry. But in fourteen months, although she won't be talking, she will be making a variety of sounds that are different from crying.

Again, something is programmed into your child's system, and that is biological development. It derives from genes and chromosomes, and accounts for a variety of changes you'll observe, including the growth of your baby's brain. It also accounts for all physical growth in your baby. Her liver grows, her other organs as well.

Most important, from my point of view as a psychiatrist, is the slow development of what we call "the voluntary musculature," those movements that your baby can make and muscle systems she can control on her own.

When you reach into your baby's crib during the first few months, holding out a rattle, the baby will respond to it, follow it with her eyes, but she cannot reach up and grab it. Somewhere around the twelfth week, she will. That's not a reaction you can teach her. Growth of cognition in the brain and the ability of the child to assimilate what's going on around her are very important for psychological growth.

The latest research shows that infants are very active, even if their style is passive. Your baby can't get up, run around, and play games with you, but she can absorb what's going on around her. She is like a sponge, especially alert when she is awake.

Watch your baby. She follows you and your movements with her eyes. Sounds startle her. She is absorbing data from her environment from the very beginning, and apparently, her brain is collecting memory traces.

That's what you'll see for the first six weeks to three months. At about three months, you'll probably notice quite a change. At that point, if a researcher recorded an EEG (an electroencephalogram), which reflects brain waves, you would find quite a remarkable change: Her brain activity has increased. Some research indicates that she is now beginning to lay down memory traces as an act of learning.

Later on, there's a nice game you can play with your baby to see for yourself when she is beginning to have a memory. I call it Playing Piaget because the game is actually an experiment Piaget used.

Take a block and hold it in front of your baby. If she is around ten months old, give or take a month or two, she'll focus on it, but if you put it under the blanket right next to her, she's lost. She can't figure out what's happened to it, has no memory of it, and forgets it right away. Then, when she's a year old, if you play the same little game, she'll begin to look around for the block. She has a memory of it. By the end of twelve months, if you don't make the game too hard, she'll probably find the block.

INHERITED CHARACTERISTICS

When your baby is out there in the nursery of the hospital, relatives and friends will play the universal game of guessing who he or she looks like. We all accept the idea that physical characteristics are inherited.

Less widely understood is the idea that your baby is not only inheriting your eyes and your husband's smile but also a temperament. It's important that you grasp this, or you might misread your baby altogether.

There are such things as passive, cooing, cooperative babies. There are also intense babies—aggressive, highly active, intense reactors; every little touch makes them jump. Your baby's particular temperament is essentially the luck of the genetic draw.

Try to recognize that and not feel guilty if, for example, you have what is called a "hard to manage" child. The child's difficult and trying temperament has not evolved that way because of something damaging you did to him. The temperament was beyond your control, though there will be ways you can affect and alter it, and normally, he will learn to manage his irritability with time.

Substantial research on inherited temperament has been conducted in the last thirty years, much of it by Stella Chess, with whom I was associated, and Alexander Thomas. They studied a large population of babies, followed them through years of growth and development, and are still tracking them. Their elegant studies were published in the mid-1970s, and have since been corroborated by a number of other people.

Chess and Thomas found that there are nine inborn functions of temperament:

1. Activity level: The newborn has either a high or low activity level.

2. Rhythmicity: The baby has a biologic rhythm, and it is either regular, variable, or irregular.

3. Approach and withdraw phenomenon: Babies reveal this from the first day of birth. If stimulated by light or noise, the baby will either approach the stimulus or withdraw from it.

4. Adaptability: If there is a new sound or phenomenon in the environment, some children will adapt to it quickly, others won't and are disturbed by it.

5. Threshold of responsiveness: The baby is either highly responsive to what's going on around it or requires quite a bit of stimulation before it notices what's happening.

6. Quality of mood: Is the baby usually in a positive mood or negative mood whenever something happens

to it or around it? Some babies possess a negative mood; whatever happens to them, they will cry.

7. Distractability: A baby might be distracted easily if several things are going on, or might focus on one thing and stay focused.

8. Attention span and persistence: How long the baby will stick with a stimulus.

9. Intensity: The baby will have either a strong re-action or a mild reaction to stimuli and environment.

From these studies, Chess and Thomas also developed three general personality types—easy children, slow-to-warm-up children, and difficult children—categories that are more controversial than the nine inborn characteristics. Still, I find their observations useful.

Easy Children

They discovered that 40 percent of the children they studied were "easy children": their rhythms were regular, they were positive approachers, they showed a high adaptability to change, and they exhibited mild or moderately intense moods that were preponderately positive.

During the first two to twelve weeks, these children develop a regular schedule, a consistent rhythm. They sleep about the same amount of time every day, show hunger at about the same time each day. You will come to bless that relative regularity, and indeed will adjust your own biological rhythms to match.

Slow-to-Warm-Up Children

About 15 percent of Chess and Thomas's group were "slow-to-warm-up children." They showed mildly negative responses to new stimuli, slow adaptability after repeated contact, and they tended to need a good bit of time before their various responses shifted from negative to positive, before they became comfortable in new situations.

In infancy, these children don't present many difficulties, but as they grow up they do have some problems. They might, for example, find it harder to be left alone, to go to new places, to make friends and play with other children, to learn. So, if you're aware that your child is a slow-to-warm-up type you wouldn't throw her into a party and leave. Nor would you scold her for crying in such situations and tell her she's simply got to try to get along better with other children.

She is not retarded or abnormal or damaged, but she has a particular personality and you have to adjust for it. Often, all such a child needs to overcome what is for her a threatening situation is for her mother or father to stay with her a while. That is not a lot to ask or expect, so long as you understand your child's problem.

Difficult Children

About 10 percent of the group were irregular in biological functions and manifested negative withdrawal, nonadaptability, or slow adaptability associated with an intense mood. Usually they are nasty and intensely irritable.

These "difficult children" have irregular sleep and feeding patterns, slow acceptance of new foods, and prolonged adjustment periods to new routines, situations, and people. They are also given fairly often to loud periods of crying, and any kind of minimum frustration leads to tantrums. They even seem to be easily irritated when you cuddle them. Some cry no matter what you do, even if you feed them or simply hold them.

This baby reacts intensely to everything in her environment. Sometimes called "colicky" when she overreacts to her digestive processes, she also overreacts to her teething process and everything around her.

Unfortunately, this difficult-to-manage baby, as she is also called, will stay this way for anywhere from six weeks to six months, pretty much no matter what you or your pediatrician does. Some difficult traits will remain for years. Put simply, this baby is tough and tiring to live with, and terribly frustrating. Typically, when the baby is somewhere around three months old you'll throw up your hands. No matter what you do, this baby will not sleep or eat on any schedule, seems to have bad tummy aches, and cries and cries for no apparent reason. You will almost certainly decide you've got to be doing something wrong, terribly wrong.

If your baby turns out this way, try to understand that you are not a bad parent, only an unlucky one, and that this too shall pass. In the meantime, try not to get chronically angry with him. The infant, like you, is blameless, no more responsible for his fits of screaming than for his blue eyes. Try to be patient during this time and comfort your child as much as you possibly can. It is difficult and trying, but I have found that in such cases understanding what is happening is in itself a help to parents, and with that knowledge they both make extra efforts to support each other.

About 65 percent of the children studied are in these three categories. The other 35 percent exhibit an amalgam of variable amounts of the nine biological givens of temperament that Chess and Thomas identified.

Whichever traits your baby shows, don't be overly concerned. She will grow through some, while others you can alter. That is part of what parenting is all about: influencing your child's psychology and development, helping your child modify certain psychological givens, teaching her new ways to adapt to her culture and get along in the world.

There are two ways in which people modify themselves. One is beyond the reach of your infant: complicated problem solving. People do change by gaining insight into themselves, coming to understand their problem and coping with it. But your child will not have the ability to do that until she is six or older.

The other way is by learning a specific set of rules, the do's and don'ts of our culture. They will come from you and your husband, and as your child copes and follows them she will be adapting and modifying herself.

By becoming a good observer of your child and getting to know her well, you'll be able to help her learn and change more efficiently.

PSYCHOLOGICAL DEVELOPMENT

This is where the biological elements we've just been considering come together with the cultural—and where you as a parent come together with your baby as a primary shaping force.

Freud viewed the Ego, or the conscious mind, as the great moderator between the internal mirror, the Unconscious, and the external, cultural environment, represented by the Superego. The Superego will become important to your child as a kind of repository of guidelines, of cultural norms and right and wrong.

The Unconscious for Freud included the biological and a great swelter of primitive needs and primitive wants, that responded according to a simple rule: the pleasure principle. Babies are happiest, he decided, when their mouths are stimulated. They get their earliest and strongest gratification, and thereby pleasure, by oral gratification. While I don't hold with everything Freud postulated, I think the pleasure principle does illuminate much of a child's behavior.

Your baby's needs are very basic. She wants to fill her tummy. She wants to get rid of her dirty diapers. She wants to feel warm and comfortable. She wants to feel loved. And that's pretty much it. Those are her unconscious drives, and so long as you satisfy those needs, she's going to survive.

Though Freud considered other issues in infants, he thought the pleasure principle was deep and primary in them. Indeed, babies do put everything into their mouths. And in recent years, neurophysiologists who map the brain and its functions have found that in newborns the most fully developed part of the brain is that related to the mouth.

It seems to me that, in this area of oral sexuality, Freud is widely misunderstood. He didn't mean that children are all sexed up. He simply meant that they, and we, get pleasure from our mouths. Babies are helpless, oral little creatures, under the mandate of their biology, and that mandate is clearly to stay fed in order to remain alive, find love, and grow. There's no survival without orality. You have to get food into your mouth.

Take this a step further. Psychoanalysts attach a lot of pathology to this area of oral pleasure, and we don't have to examine all that. But there are elements that are useful. For example, Freud felt that if you were terribly deprived as a child, and here he meant deprived of both food and emotional input for a long period of time, you would develop into the kind of person who has a strong need to take a great deal from other people.

Erik Erikson elaborated on that. Psychologically, you will have the need to take from other people, he said. But in addition, if you don't receive enough emotional input or motor stimulation or appropriate feeding over time, you become distrustful of your environment. Yet, in order for a person to function properly and survive in a culture, he has to trust other people. This means that in order for your baby to start trusting his environment, he must have some predictability in his life. He must be fed and clothed and held and stimulated often and regularly. He must receive a lot of emotional and physical stimulation from you, your husband, your surrogate, the rest of your immediate family. Whenever he is awake, he needs to know that the world is predictable.

Does that mean that every time he makes a peep he must have a breast or a bottle in his mouth? Absolutely not. Life forces us to learn to tolerate a little frustration.

Let's talk about this matrix where psychological theory and practical parenting come together.

Your baby starts to cry, a sound that is an alarm in your home. You bolt, or maybe it's your husband's turn. He sits up, and before he's even opened his eyes, he's got his slippers and robe on.

Your responses are the normal ones of new parents who want to give their baby all they can.

Yet nothing will happen to the infant if he has to wait five minutes, maybe ten minutes. In fact, he might just go back to sleep. And if he doesn't go back to sleep, if he's really hungry, that delay and the frustration he feels at being denied his instant oral gratification can be a good thing. He is beginning to develop frustration tolerance.

I don't mean to overdo this. Don't let him howl for half an hour. Five minutes for a baby in his first year of life can be a long time. And during his first three months, you might not want to try this at all. You're still feeling out his rhythms and patterns during that period. As you go along, you'll want to adjust your delays to your child's evolving rhythm and schedule. If it's clear that he's starving around two every morning, that's one call you want to respond to quickly.

These delays can also help you regularize his rhythms, get him to grasp that during certain times you're more responsive than others.

From the start, set up two time zones: light responsive and dark responsive. During the day, the light zone, try being a bit more responsive to his cries. At night, take your time a little more. He might get the message and associate light with fairly instant gratification, dark with less gratification.

None of this, by the way, interferes with demand feeding—feeding the baby whenever he seems to demand it—if you want to do that rather than scheduled feeding. Demand feeding does not mean instantaneous feeding.

So far as the psychological benefits go, there's no proof that one feeding system is better for the baby than the other. There are cultures that start out training a baby to eat on schedule with considerable success and no known mass psychological havoc.

It's probably somewhat better for the baby if you do accommodate his demand pattern at first. Most people, I think, will go along with demand feeding for four to six weeks, hoping that the baby will regularize during that period. Actually, by the end of a month you can begin to train the baby. His biology is resilient enough to take feedings on schedule rather than on demand.

Let me remind you again that your baby is not trying to be mean to you or manipulate you with all his crying and his demands. At this stage of life he has no intent, good or bad. He's just responding to all those basic needs, his drive for instant gratification, his pleasure principle.

BASIC TRUST VERSUS BASIC DISTRUST

I spoke earlier of the importance of the baby's trusting his environment, and you might wonder if that trust won't be undermined, if not shattered, by frustration delays.

There's an important distinction here. In fact, babies are resilient enough to tolerate a certain amount of frustration. It is what happens beyond that point that can be critical. In other words, repetitive deprivation, extended and continuous deprivation, is going to erode personality development. Long-term deprivation is the most common problem I face in hospitals and clinics in children of this age group.

. I call this period, from birth to fourteen months, the Age of Dependency. And it is a period when trust is the most important issue, a time when there is a kind of balancing of basic trust versus basic distrust.

Basic trust evolves in part from that predictability in the environment I spoke of, from a certain amount of warmth, love, and stimulation, from being reasonably well clothed, well housed. Life should seem decent to your infant, the world a pretty good place, even to a helpless organism. If she lies endlessly hungry in her filth, she will not find life very comforting.

Basic trust, as opposed to trust in general, is something that develops between your baby and you, your baby and your husband and maybe one or two other adults. Much of it is rooted in love. It is the quality that enables a child to respond to you and essentially do as you say, even if it curtails her pleasure. She gives up something she would rather do in the hope and expectation of an exchange with you. She behaves, in other words, out of love for Mommy and Daddy. In the best of all worlds, that would be sufficient every time you asked something of her. In the real world, as we'll see, you'll have to call upon all levels of rewards and disciplinary techniques in addition to love and this basic trust.

Basic trust is also the quality of love and bonding that enables you to teach her. She places her trust in you for that act.

As we'll see, it's important that this basic trust develops during this first stage of life, from birth to fourteen months, when the infant is a dependent creature. Because somewhere toward the end of this period there is a biological change that makes her much less dependent and alters everything. She starts to walk. The ability to walk makes her capable of doing countless things that were beyond her power before. And you will have to tell her not to do many of those things with requests and commands that can be effective if she trusts you.

In order for the basic trust to develop between you and your child during this period, she has to sense that you are telling her the truth, that she is getting "accurate data" from you and her environment. Accurate data for her means being reasonably well taken care of in all the ways we've discussed and having objects around her—people being objects to her—who are reasonably responsive and loving.

Basic trust evolves out of "object relations," in which you and she interact in a way that gives each of you a sense of yourself but also creates something special between the two of you. This is "bonding," and from it your baby will begin to feel that you, your husband, your surrogate, are special. And she'll do special things for you because you are. It's not a conscious thought for her at this point, though it becomes conscious later on. For now it is unconscious, and it prompts her to respond to you.

If your child doesn't trust you and the other objects in her environment, she won't respond appropriately to the rules and regulations you convey to her and which she needs if she's going to be culturally organized in our society.

If she does trust you, she will respond, and she'll begin to sense, as her little life develops, that things are changing. That once upon a time the environment around her provided everything. Food appeared magically. Personal care and love came in exchange for nothing. But now, with the passing of a little time, the environment will still provide love and all those nice things, though not quite so magically. They will be provided in exchange for certain kinds of behavior, called "being good." And "being good" is really abiding by cultural norms.

It becomes an exchange between a small organism and another, larger organism. For changing her behavior, for curtailing her pleasure principle, she will receive love, food, shelter, stimulation.

As you can begin to see, this is the foundation of

discipline and limit setting, which we'll discuss at length in the next chapter.

It is what the next stage of your relationship—that period from fourteen to thirty months, when your child can walk—will be based upon. I call it the Age of Exploration because that's what she's doing: locomoting all over the place by herself, exploring her universe. A great time for her, but a time, obviously, when the two of you need that bond and deep trust to draw upon as well.

HOW YOUR BABY LEARNS ABOUT HIS ENVIRONMENT

Later in this chapter we'll discuss what a dreadful idea it is to try to turn your infant into a genius. If you smother your baby in "learning objects" and shatter his calm with a tape recorder that's blaring the alphabet, he'll reject all that false stimulation.

However, even without such intrusive stimulation, he's learning prodigiously during these months. His brain has a basic biological need to lay down data, his earliest memory traces. It's what Piaget called "assimilation," and your baby is continually assimilating.

There's a kind of two-way street operating here. As the brain develops, it assimilates. Then it accommodates—adjusts according to what it has assimilated and integrates the data it has received.

The brain must be working, it must be receiving from you, at least in the baby's waking moments, to stimulate its development. This is a good example of nature and nurture operating, as they do in so much of child development.

Earlier, we considered the need for real stimulation. For our purposes, real stimulation means any kind of close involvement and interaction with the baby, and that includes holding, cuddling, talking, making faces, and all those other similar silly things grown-ups do with babies. The need is great. In fact, in extreme cases, babies left alone and not stimulated will either die or become retarded. Without stimulation and interaction, their brains are deprived of sufficient input. They don't have enough memory data to develop normally.

As your baby's waking periods grow longer, you and your husband and surrogate will have the job of interacting more and more with her and of providing more toys and things for her to play and interact with.

Don't feel you ought to wake your baby up for extra stimulation. Apparently, during the first twelve weeks of life, the baby's immature brain can take only so much action. Then it gets fatigued, and brain and baby want to rest. Let the baby's natural rhythms tell you when she wants more heady stuff.

The more your baby's brain develops and the more she is stimulated, the wider her concentration span seems to become. Some of that process is automatic, some is a result of the environment you're creating—again, nature and nurture.

There are automatic changes and developments you can anticipate, though I urge you not to chart them.

I mentioned the dramatic change that comes at around three months that would be reflected in an EEG. At that point, the brain has grown enough so that your baby begins to get better coordinated.

Somewhere around then, or a bit before, she will show you her "social smile." You and your husband will, of course, think your child is finally recognizing you both and telling you how pleased she is with everything you've done. Not quite, though you can still enjoy her first smiles. Actually, she is responding to faces—any face will do, even a horrible mask. She is also responding to movement. So if you put on the worst Halloween mask and move toward her, she'll smile back.

She is also beginning to leave the world that Margaret Mahler, the foremost researcher of separation and individuation, called "autistic." The autistic child is totally into herself, just a biological organism. She develops from autistic to "symbiotic." She goes from being in a world of her own to being in a world where she is related to something and living off it. You'll know that's happening when you see your baby grabbing your glasses a lot and always looking into things. She's beginning to sense that she's a piece of an environment, no longer only taking in, but not yet actively interacting either.

Somewhere between three and eight or nine months, she'll get enough of a memory trace to differentiate between a face that's recognizable, safe, and friendly and one that is not. That's the phenomenon called "stranger anxiety."

When she cries as her grandmother comes into the room, that's what is happening. Though your mother might be slightly hurt by the greeting, nothing personal is intended. She is simply a strange, unfamiliar face to your baby. The baby has sufficient memory at this stage to relate to something good about a face, and is able to think to herself: "That face [yours] is good. That other face [your mother's] . . . well, nobody knows what that face is. It sure isn't good."

This stage usually doesn't last more than a few weeks, and with children who have several surrogates the response is usually very mild.

Related to this behavior is the "white coat syndrome." Your baby is beginning to realize that doctors don't always do nice things, and your pediatrician's face becomes the nasty face. Later, after that data is assimilated, the doctor becomes the one who gives the injections. (This is why many psychologically aware doctors now ask assistants and nurses to give shots.)

So, with "stranger anxiety" we see memory traces; soon we'll see something more. Your baby's motor system is responding to something that is coming in. She moves past the stage of "see glasses, grab glasses" to "see the person, remember something good about the person, compare that memory with the person." That is assimilated data being used. Somehow, her brain is automatically comparing the "good" with the person, or with a new thing out there. If the stimulus is not the same as the memory, that means danger. This is a pretty good built-in biologic reflex: what is not recognized is unpleasurable, and what is different is dangerous. Assimilation in action.

THE BEGINNINGS OF SEPARATION

"Where is that girl? Where did that little girl go?" you are saying as, for the ninth time, she ducks behind the drapes. "Oh, there she is!" you cry as she pops out once again, absolutely beaming.

The game, of course, is peekaboo, but in your child's mind something more than fun is going on. She is "practicing," seeing what happens if she disappears from your sight. Will you vanish?

This is all part, around fourteen months, of the beginnings of "separation anxiety." She is starting to explore her environment and needs to reassure herself. If she goes into the other room to play, she'll keep coming back to the living room, where you're reading. Maybe come over and touch you. Back to the other room, soon returning to you. Back and forth.

After a while, she'll be able to handle the separation for longer and longer periods. It's called "rapprochement," and it lasts until she's about three. Indeed, many people feel that a child is not comfortable being totally separated from a parent and/or a close surrogate much before three.

That seems to be when she possesses a sense of individuation, when she can say to herself that she is separate from her parents and yet is able to cope with that ominous idea, partly because she is able to maintain an image of her parents in her head. That is "object constancy.'' She carries in her head the memory of you, your husband, maybe your surrogate as well, in a way that conveys to her a feeling of safety and eventually allows her to separate from you. As we'll see later in the book, if she goes off into a room full of children at nursery school, for example, and you leave her, she can cope. She knows you will not disappear forever.

THE REAL WORLD

Let's examine common problems, concerns, and everyday dilemmas of this stage. A certain amount of the material in this chapter relates to the experiences and stresses of first-time parents: settling, for example, the question of breast-feeding, or the amount of time you should take off from work after having your baby. If you already have had a child, you may well have resolved such matters. Other parts of the discussion are broader: the important subject of sexual identity and sexual roles, for example, or how to interpret your child's rate of development. Some material overlaps the particular interests of first-time parents and those of parents adding to their families: postpartum blues, for example, which affects all new mothers.

POSTPARTUM BLUES

You have had your baby, and it is healthy, maybe even the sex you wanted, and you are ecstatic in a way you've never known before.

You are also whipped, unbelievably fatigued; your body has suddenly lost pounds and pounds—the baby and all the support systems that went with her—and your system is shifting hormonally from a state of pregnancy to one of normalcy.

Before long you will most likely find yourself feeling down, experiencing postpartum blues. This has nothing to do with the more famous postpartum depression, a severe psychiatric condition with long-term consequences. This is a letdown that will last a couple of weeks.

A number of elements feed this feeling, despite the transcendent joyousness of the moment. First of all, you've had a tremendous drain on your physical system, and you are worn out. For nine months you carried the fetus around, and then you experienced the effort of childbirth itself. And childbirth, even the most natural delivery, is hard work. Both you and your husband will feel something of a deflation after all those months of tension, the worries about having a healthy baby, the special stresses of the last three months of your pregnancy.

An added source of anxiety for some parents can be the fact that a baby might not look very pretty in the first few days after he's born. Having just come through the physical rigors of birth, he may be wrinkled, blotched, scraggly—hardly the glowing, model infant of your fantasies.

What makes matters worse is that there's much more work and anxiety in those first weeks than you ever anticipated. During the first two weeks, the infant's every face movement, every cry, will create panic. And that will add to a sense of oppressiveness. After all, when people are inexperienced, they tend to be overanxious, overfrightened. And that's you and your husband, totally new at this job of parenting and completely fearful that this tiny being might break if you drop it, or choke if you feed it the wrong way. In fact, in a way your baby is more durable at this stage of things than you are, though I don't think it would help much to remind you of the millions of infants who are basically dropped in the fields and survive quite well. But if you and your husband, in your overanxious state, have difficulty sleeping or eating well, you will wear yourselves out that much more.

Oddly, it won't help that you're coming from a hospital setting, where the baby has been taken care of twenty-four hours a day by professionals. Now you and your husband have to do it all alone, and neither of you has even changed a diaper before. I have a friend who confessed that he was almost hysterical because his wife was about to be discharged with their baby and they hadn't been taught by the hospital how to give a bath.

These anxieties and the blues will pass. But perhaps you can see why it is a very good idea if your husband is able to take a week or two off from work to be home at the start, and why you should have some special help, a relative or hired person, for this tough time.

BREAST-FEEDING

People who favor breast-feeding tend to be extremely passionate about it and make sweeping claims for its physical and psychological benefits for mothers and their nursing infants. One result of this is that women who don't plan to breast-feed, generally working mothers, get worried and feel guilty about their decision. There really is no need for great concern, one way or the other.

Biologically, a certain amount of passive immunity is conveyed by breast-feeding. Yet, modern medicine renders that a relatively insignificant matter, surely no longer a necessity in advanced countries.

Psychologically, whether you breast-feed or bottle-feed doesn't make a bit of difference, so long as you do more than stuff the bottle in your baby's mouth, if you choose to feed that way.

Feeding should be a time for coddling and jiggling and stimulating the baby. That happens rather naturally if you breast-feed, and, of course, you will have a great feeling of closeness merely because your bodies are joined together. While all of that is psychologically satisfying to the baby, it can all be achieved with a bottle—

if you make the effort with smiles and songs and cuddling.

It is, obviously, quite inconvenient to be working and breast-feeding, though you can breast-pump yourself and leave a few feedings in the refrigerator before you go off to the office.

Is a compromise like that worth the effort? Yes, if it means a lot to you. So far as the baby is concerned, as I said, breast or bottle will make little difference. But if breast-feeding gives you great satisfaction, do it.

You should forget about breast-feeding, however, if you're a drug or alcohol abuser. Keep your poisons to yourself and feed with a bottle.

WORKING MOTHER ANGST

I don't think I've ever met a working mother who didn't feel guilty about being away from her baby. The effects are greatly debated, of course, and although I respect some of the arguments for staying home and being a full-time mother, I have yet to see convincing evidence that by being a working mother you are doing your child harm—assuming, of course, that you make the necessary substitute arrangements.

No matter how common it has become for mothers to work, no matter how good a job the mother has or how much of herself she has invested in it, she feels that her child will grow up maimed and scarred, unloved and deeply neurotic because she's not there. In short, she feels she is a terrible, selfish person, putting herself and her career ahead of her child's most basic needs.

A number of myths and fantasies get in the way here. First of all, there is the fantasy that the only committed mother is the full-time mother. The fact is, if you look at most societies around the world, the full-time mother barely exists. Almost all mothers have to work. They might go to fields rather than offices, but they do work and they have always worked.

And what happens to their children? They have surrogate mothers to take care of them. Traditionally, families called on Grandma or Auntie, some woman who was no longer able to work actively. Most cultures, quite simply, could not afford to have able-bodied women stay at home.

Now talk of surrogates raises other fantasy fears. "How will my baby know me, know I'm her mother, if I'm not there, if some other woman is with her all day? Won't that other woman replace me in my baby's affections?" That's how one working mother put it.

The fact is that within twelve weeks your baby will be able to identify you as one of her primary caregivers. It is part of the bonding process. And from twelve weeks to eight months your baby will discern who its parents are and which other people it can trust. Babies and, as we'll see, infants and young children make distinctions between real parents and housekeepers or surrogate parents. They develop quite different relationships with their surrogates. So there really is no need for real or imagined competition between you and someone you hire to replace you during the day.

However, if you are going to be a working mother, and if, as is most likely, your husband works also, you both should expect to make an extra effort to stay in touch with your baby.

This might mean that you establish special times for baby. Perhaps early in the morning for a fun feeding or fun bathing, and maybe when you come home at night for a special playtime. Such an effort will help establish the rapport between you two and baby that you both want, and it will also help alleviate your anxiety about your baby's relating only to your housekeeper.

"HOW MUCH TIME SHOULD I TAKE OFF FROM MY JOB?"

A tough, common, and very important question asked by all working mothers.

I recommend three months as a reasonable minimum and six months as a reasonable ideal.

As I noted, chances are that for the first two weeks after you deliver the baby you're going to be in a slump, physically and mentally—the postpartum blues. So, you won't feel like running back to your office or doing too much of anything.

Once you feel more like normal, give yourself and your baby a chance to get to know each other. You owe that to yourself. If you have only one child, those first weeks and months will be unlike any other in your life.

I also think that spending those first months with the baby lessens that obligatory guilt I mentioned. If you are burdened that way, even after my admonitions that the guilt is unwarranted, at least you'll be able to say to yourself: "I got that child off to the right start."

You can also get your surrogate off to the right start during this time by bringing her in to work during your last two to four weeks at home (four is better than two, but it is also twice as expensive). This is a perfect chance to show her how you want her to feed your baby and play with her, and it will help you confirm that you've selected the right person. If you have confidence in this new and essential person in your life, it will do a great deal to dissolve your natural anxiety (and guilt) about leaving your baby with a relative stranger when you do go back to work.

(By the way, nothing I know of says your caregiver must be a woman. But it is highly unlikely in our culture that you would choose a man, even though I have seen capable men working in day-care centers.)

I also recommend that husbands take off two weeks to a month and stay home, both to support their wives and to learn what a baby is all about. (There is some data that the earlier the father becomes involved with the baby the more he seems able to adapt to baby and child care.)

If you can have additional help, beyond your husband, during those first hard two weeks, get it. It might be your mother or some other relative, if you're comfortable having them around. Or you can hire a special baby nurse, though they can be quite expensive. The idea is to have someone who can share some of the very tiring work of caring for a newborn on a demanding timetable—and help with other household chores as well.

If you simply cannot be away from your job for more than two or three weeks, as some women cannot, it will not be catastrophic for your baby, provided you do some planning. Most especially, you should spend as much high-quality time with the baby as you possibly can manage—mornings, nights, and weekends, when you're not working—and make every effort to choose the right surrogate to maintain your child's environment in your absence. (We'll consider high-quality time at length in the next chapter.)

WHAT YOU WANT IN A CAREGIVER

You want someone you can trust, someone who is responsible, if possible someone experienced in raising children, her own or someone else's. Warmth and a rapport with children are important; genius is not. The caregiver does have to be smart and observant enough to follow your orders, interact with your child, and fill you in at the end of each day about what's been happening. But you should not expect the person to speak six languages, play the piano, and love Mozart or be current on the latest theories of child development.

Someone warm, kind, and trustworthy is sufficient. Make it your job to do the rest. There is confusion among many parents on this issue, and they expect far too much intellectual competence of their housekeepers. If you want your baby exposed to Mozart, which is rather idiotic to begin with, simply tell your surrogate to play certain tapes and records. More important, if you think your baby is not getting enough stimulation from the woman, then talk to her. Explain why it's important to have certain kinds of play going on and how often you expect it. You could have hired a woman who comes from a culture where such things are not stressed at all, but that doesn't mean she can't follow your instructions and provide them. What you cannot teach her is to be caring, warm, gentle, and affectionate, and your baby needs those elements much more than Mozart.

How do you know if a woman has these qualities? Ultimately, by watching her—which is why that training period, during those first three months after delivery, when you're still at home, is so critical.

Of course, you will get your first sense of her when you do your interviewing for the job, which should be somewhere around your sixth or seventh month of pregnancy. After you meet and interview her, check her references, talk with the women she previously worked for, and you'll be able to judge her.

You should then begin to be comfortable with her, and I mean ''comfortable'' in a complex way: You can communicate with her and you feel she is someone you can trust with your baby. It takes a highly accomplished psychopath to make you comfortable and then deceive you. There are such con artists, but chances are that if you do feel comfortable with a woman, your sense of trust in her will not be misplaced.

It's important for husbands to be involved in these interviews, which might seem too obvious to mention, yet even these days they often don't participate. Frequently, a man doesn't stop to think that he's going to be living with this woman in your home, so from that perspective, as well as the broader matters of trustworthiness and the other factors we're discussing, his responses and feelings are important.

In the end, you should make your decision about the woman after watching her work. You wouldn't hire someone to work in your office without some sort of probation period, so don't do it with your surrogate.

Watch how she behaves with your baby. What are her style and temperament? How does she respond to your instructions? Have her do some shopping to see how she copes with a new neighborhood. Go out yourself for a couple of hours so you can see how she's doing with the baby on her own when you return.

After a week, you will probably know if she is right for you and if your original feeling of comfort was well placed. Indeed, it should have grown. I think you can imagine how much better you're going to feel when you go back to work in another two or three weeks, knowing you're going to feel secure about your surrogate. Think of that, as opposed to how anxious you would be if you hired someone on Sunday and rushed back to the office on Monday.

Even if you do have a successful trial period and feel very good about your new caregiver, you will undoubtedly still have some nervousness. Whether such worries are well founded or not, it's probably a good idea to go home at lunchtime once or twice a week at first to see how things are going, that the house isn't in chaos, that the nurse isn't fulfilling your darkest worries by having some kind of orgy in the living room while your baby howls in its crib. And call once a day to get the latest news from her.

What happens if she doesn't work out? Fire her and try someone else.

There is often concern on the part of parents about letting caregivers go after their infants have formed some attachment. I don't recommend weekly replacements, but in fact, trying out three or four women during the baby's first eight or nine months is not going to make any hurtful difference to the child. Only around the eighth month does the baby begin to discriminate among its caregivers, sorting out the safe ones from the others. However, if you can settle on one woman during the first six months, so much the better.

A surrogate would need to be involved with your baby for three to three and a half months for the relationship to be significant to your baby, and you should be able to decide how you feel about her before then.

Older babies, after nine or ten months, are capable of forming a real relationship with a caregiver. Then, after the baby is about a year old, there is an attachment that can be tough on the baby when it's broken. (This is magnified as the child grows, which we'll discuss later in the book.) But most children can tolerate losing a surrogate, provided their home is organized in a reasonable, supportive way and remains intact. Still, the preferred thing, once you have found someone satisfactory for the job, is for you both to think in terms of a long-term commitment. Your chances for that will improve if you can avoid having unreal expectations of your surrogate. Remember, it is a job for her; this is not her own child. She is there for money. You are paying her for responsibility, trustworthiness, warmth, real caring, and good instincts.

DAY CARE

Many parents, of course, cannot afford to have a caregiver in their home for their child. The question I get asked most often about the day-care alternative is: "Am I hurting my child by putting her into a day-care center?"

The answer is no, with some ifs and buts.

I have to assume, first of all, that the center you put the child into is state certified, sanctioned by some legitimate philanthropic organization, or, if private, has an affiliation with a high-quality organization such as a hospital.

It should have a ratio of no more than three children to every surrogate—better is two to one. You're trading individual care for multiple surrogates. If the ratio is no more than three to one, your child might have to put up with a bit of frustration, and might not receive all the stimulation you'd like and would get with your own housekeeper, but there should be no harm done to the child.

Studies of kibbutzes in Israel and well organized day-care programs show they can be reasonably equal to individual care and certainly not damaging to the children.

I am not speaking of the many black market day-care programs—a woman taking in six or eight children to watch for the day. That is not care, but garaging, and it's bad for your baby.

The ideal solution is to have a day-care center where you work, so you can pop in on your breaks and lunches. A few companies, hospitals, and colleges are trying this, but it's still quite rare in the United States.

If you don't have a day-care program that meets the proper standards and is convenient, you have still another alternative to an expensive surrogate: be old-fashioned and have a relative take care of your baby while you work.

Mothers and mothers-in-law who get along well with children can help you enormously. But be careful that the two of you agree on what to do. If you have vastly different views on child rearing, obviously you are only inviting major clashes.

Also, be sure they really want to do it. You can't impose the job on them—and it certainly is a job. Bear in mind, there's nothing worse than a reluctant baby-sitter.

REORGANIZING YOUR WORLD

From the moment your doctor gave you the news and confirmed your pregnancy, your life changed. From that historic moment, you and your husband have to make some adaptations.

Being parents will mean some sacrifices, changes in life-style, though I hope I make clear throughout this book that you will not and should not give up all the pleasures of life for your baby. Resentful parents do not make good parents, and it's important that you continue to do the things you enjoy, even make a conscious effort to do them. (We'll talk later about things like "parents' night out" and your vacation away from baby.)

But as I said earlier, giving up certain pleasures such as smoking and drinking are sacrifices you'll have to make when you're pregnant. I don't know a reputable gynecologist/obstetrician today who doesn't insist that his pregnant patients stop smoking. The carbon monoxide that you inhale when you smoke can compromise brain development in your baby.

Some doctors allow a glass of wine a day, nothing stronger; some say stop drinking altogether. Of course, drugs of all kinds are out.

Once your baby is born, healthier for your abstinence, you might want to consider extending your period of good behavior, at least in part, for the first six years of your child's life. Aside from the fact that smoking can kill you, you should know that somewhere around your child's second year of life he is going to begin to model himself on you and your husband. If you want your child to be a smoker, all you have to do is smoke around the house. You've educated another smoker.

A number of women have told me they welcomed their obstetrician's order as just the push they needed to finally give up cigarettes once and for all. And they do it, too. Others, of course, go back to it after the baby is born.

More common is a return to moderate drinking. I'm a wine lover, so I can deeply empathize with that sacrifice. In terms of your child, without making a federal case of this, remember that you are a model.

REORGANIZE YOUR GEOGRAPHY

Figure out where your baby is going to live in your apartment or house. I'm well aware of the space limitations in city apartments these days, and there's no big problem if during his first year he shares your bedroom. But after that time, the baby will become intrusive, and it will be better psychologically for the baby to have a space of his own. It also simplifies life greatly.

You've heard about the terrible trauma that befalls a baby sleeping in the same room as its parents? The famous "primal scene," when the baby wakes up and sees and hears her parents having intercourse, which to the baby appears to be some terrible fight between the two of you? Generally, we used to think that such a moment was significant in the infant's psychological development. But as we have learned more about how and what they can learn and absorb, the importance of this during the first nine or ten months has diminished. Some Freudians still argue its meaningful impact. I was trained as a Freudian, but on this and many other points, I now have a different view.

The evidence today does not convince me that there is danger of trauma here during the first months. Still, I think discretion is the better part of valor, and common sense should prevail. I have heard of parents screening off a section of their bedroom for the baby's crib. I have heard of others going to the living room when they wanted to make love.

After ten or eleven months, your child is at a much

more highly developed state, and I would provide her
with her own living space.

SEXUAL IDENTITY, SEXUAL ROLES

The whole business of sexual identity and sexual roles
is a cultural subject that is much discussed these days
and much misunderstood. Put simply, if you have a
little girl, does it matter if she wears blue instead of
pink? Does it matter if your little boy plays with dolls?

No, to both those questions. Cultural frills don't matter. What does matter is how you relate to your child
in terms of being a little boy or little girl, helping them
identify themselves sexually. They should know what
they are. From the beginning, you should be calling
your little boy a little boy, your little girl a little girl.
By the time they are two, they will know pretty well
what they are, and between two and three their sexual
identities will be clearly formed.

Helping them grasp their sexuality does not mean—
and here is where so much confusion comes in—that
you will be transmitting stereotyped messages about the
sexes. There is a profound difference between sexual
identity and sexual roles.

Sexual identity is what you help your child absorb,
an inner core and sense of self that allows her or him
to be a sexual creature. A girl needs to know she's a
female, a biological female. Eventually she should know
that females bear children, that it is an appropriate part
of being female and she should feel good about the
possibility that she will bear children someday, and feed
and care for them. Whether she does or not is irrele-
vant. It has nothing to do with defining her role in the
world, nothing to do with her being a firefighter, riv-
eter, or head of a corporation.

Boys should know, with your help, that they are boys,
different from girls, and should have a sense of their
own maleness. And they will be told later on that males

impregnate women. In a Darwinian sense, that's their biological function—to propagate the race. But that has nothing to do with their role in the workplace, being kind, expressing emotions openly, or being able to cry.

For good psychological health, so far as we know, your child must have a reasonably strong sense of sexual identity to grow into a properly functioning heterosexual human being. If you bring up your child androgynously, as a neutral being, there is real doubt about whether the child will function heterosexually later on in life. Bring up a little boy as if he were a little girl and you bear the risk that he'll have sexual problems relating to women.

This is a particularly complex and confusing area of human development, and it is under continuing study. It does seem possible that if you have an effete male with a genetic predisposition to homosexuality or possibly with low testosterone, the male hormone, and raise him like a little girl, he could end up homosexual or even transsexual. But no matter how little testosterone a boy has, if you bring him up male, in all likelihood he'll remain a psychological male.

I think it's important, then, that your little boy knows what he is, and furthermore that he's proud to be a little boy. And the same for little girls.

Once again, their roles can be whatever you want them to be. All parents teach their children about different male and female roles subtly, often through toys. Boys are still in their cribs when they get baseball bats. Girls are barely born when they get dolls.

You could reverse the toys—give the girls the bats, the boys the dolls—and at this stage of life, the first fourteen months, it won't make any difference. (Later on, it is more complicated.) I can't think of a toy you could give to a boy or a girl at this stage that would disturb their sense of being a boy or a girl.

Or, you could stop worrying about male/female toys

altogether and simply give neutral toys such as rattles and blocks.

How you dress your child, however, is different.

Your daughter should learn fairly early in life, perhaps toward the end of this period, that there are things that identify her as a female. The wearing of dresses is one of them.

Her development of sexual identity and heterosexuality, and subsequently the whole issue of courtship and attachment, has various elements associated with it. Among them is attractiveness: how females attract males and males attract females later in life. And to some degree, clothing has its role in all this.

This doesn't mean that girls shouldn't wear dungarees or dress neutrally, but it may be meaningful for girls to know that in our culture there are sexual differences that are attractive to males later on.

I fear that, in the context of current debate, much of what I'm saying will be attributed to a "male chauvinist" bias. It's not intended that way. It's intended as a psychocultural observation. Other cultures have highly sexual dances, mating rituals. Women stretch their necks in parts of Africa; men wear penis sheaths in New Guinea. This is all in the name of enhancing sexuality. And at some point little girls and little boys should understand that sexuality is a legitimate part of functioning in adult life.

MY CHILD IS NOT SLEEPING. WHY? WHAT CAN I DO ABOUT IT?

This is a purely biological phenomenon. Your child's biological clock will determine whether or not he sleeps in an irregular way, or whether he sleeps when you and your husband are also sleeping. There is nothing to be alarmed about, insofar as the child's well-being is concerned. Your well-being is something else.

Earlier in this chapter, I spoke of hard-to-manage

children, and that could well be what you have. With time, your child will learn to adapt.

For now, you might try the technique I suggested of responding quickly to his cries during daylight, less quickly at night. Or even play music quietly in his room.

I am against giving the baby sedatives and other kinds of drugs, except once in a great while. If you and your husband are losing your minds along with your sleep, then, to allow yourselves a night of rest, perhaps giving him a little Benadryl or other mild antihistamine or phenobarbital for an evening is okay. Before you do, check with your pediatrician who will prescribe the appropriate amount if he or she agrees.

MY CHILD IS NOT EATING. WHY? WHAT CAN I DO ABOUT IT?

Once again, this is biologically controlled. Children tend to eat what they need.

The only time you should worry is if your child is losing weight. So long as she is gaining weight, she is eating enough, even though you may not think so. You might feel she needs all kinds of special foods because, being a good and loving mother, you want her to grow up to be as healthy as Wonder Woman. But you could be trying to feed her much more than she needs or can accept. You could be trying to prove just how much you do love and care for her, which is then your psychological problem, not her eating problem.

If she begins to lose weight for any reason, check with your pediatrician immediately.

Remember that in our society we have a great tendency to overfeed children. And there is considerable evidence that overfeeding at this stage will lead to obesity later on.

If you're breast-feeding, you'll see how your baby monitors herself. She will suck until she is full and that's it.

With bottle feeding, you'll also get a signal. If she's had enough, she'll curl up and go to sleep, and you shouldn't force her to take more. If you are truly concerned about the volume she's getting, perhaps she needs to be fed more often, but less at each feeding.

CREATING GENIUSES

We live in a culture where, it seems, parents are determined to create geniuses. The emphasis on the intellectual development of infants is very powerful—and terrific for the toy industry. You want a brilliant child, they say, fine, here are "educational toys." The result is a baby in a crib surrounded by the stuff. Overhead, he has goldfish in a plastic aquarium. On one side of his crib there's a counting toy. On the other side, a mobile. All of this because someone said stimulation will make babies smart.

True, but not that kind. Babies do need stimulation to achieve appropriate growth and development. But they need interaction with their parents, not the sterile challenge of a load of "educational toys." Just a simple rattle you shake at them and with them. Not goldfish floating overhead.

I continually see parents who get preoccupied with the developmental landmarks of their babies. When he first smiles or holds a bottle, when he stands, walks, talks. All supposedly signs of whether a new Einstein is taking shape right before their eyes.

Unfortunately, a number of the older books on child development stress these landmarks and are full of tables and charts that help you track your baby as if he were a stock on the New York Stock Exchange. We'll talk about various landmarks, but you'll notice that I have not included a single chart in this book. To my mind, all they do is make parents anxious. "Oh, my Lord, what's happening to Sam? He's four months old and he isn't smiling at me yet. He's supposed to be smiling by three months. Look at the chart. Do I have a defective child? Is he brain damaged? What have I done wrong? Haven't I stimulated him enough?''

The Wall Street Journal ran a series of articles in 1988 on working mothers and their problems. They were all highly motivated women, and they created problems that were pretty special, to say the least. One of them confessed to a fascinating guilt: she had to fly off on a business trip, missing the very week when her child's brain was most receptive to learning numbers. She had read somewhere that children's brains developed in such a way that there was one particular week when they were most fertile for the planting of numbers. And she sure wanted her child to master numbers.

What these poor parents don't understand is that each child's developmental steps are inexorably programmed. They are part of the biology of the child, and you cannot speed the process up by stimulating him. There's no evidence at all that you can make a baby smarter by teaching him the alphabet in his first year.

To the contrary, it is disastrous to overintellectualize your child. When you do that, you sacrifice the kind of input the child really needs for input that he can't integrate.

Take the alphabet. You leave the tape recorder on all day next to the crib, feeding him the ABCs. But he doesn't need or want that. He needs rest, warmth, someone to play with.

I've seen the effect of that. It's a peculiar kind of deprivation syndrome. The baby can't integrate everything coming at him. So he ends up screaming all the time. He's suffering from overstimulation, which is as bad as understimulation or the wrong kind of stimulation.

This is a period when your baby is overwhelmed by what he has to learn, tasks that might not be learning for you but are tough work for him. He has to learn all about his new environment, who his caregivers are, all about light and dark. (Think for a moment about wrestling with those two concepts.) He has to learn how to turn over. For your baby, that's the important learning process of life, not all the other intellectualization, which isn't even learning anyway.

While you are searching all around for a computer that will safely fit into the crib, try to remember what Piaget taught us. A child cannot assimilate things, knowledge, before he's ready to assimilate them. Certainly he can't assimilate what I see many parents trying to teach. Try not to get overly consumed with the teaching of things that can't be learned. You will only succeed in overloading your baby's circuits and depriving him of the real stimulation he needs.

REAL STIMULATION AND QUALITY TIME

Consider how simple and natural this real stimulation is. There are three ways you can do it.

First, by feeding her. If you hold her in your arms and cuddle her and feed her, you are stimulating her.

Second, by loving her. Holding her, patting her on the back, making all the silly, kootchie-koo sounds all parents make.

Third, by playing with her. Play is the way children learn. Again, it can be very simple and still be stimulating. Shaking a rattle at her. Holding an object over the crib and letting her follow it.

Play should be fun for both of you, but most important, it should be enjoyable for the baby. The baby shouldn't be a passive participant while you do something you want to do—like watch a football game or talk to your neighbor on the phone. Many parents don't understand this, and it's best discussed in terms of "high-quality" and "low-quality" time.

Low-quality time is doing something with your child that, in fact, is something you want to do. True, you are doing it together, but you're the one who's benefiting more, enjoying it more. Watching television with her, when it's your program. Cleaning her up. Making her go to sleep. That's all low-quality time, even if it's a necessary activity.

The ideal high-quality time is when you play with your child at something she wants to do, which is very different from playing at your game or doing something with her that has to be done anyway.

Feeding is a borderline activity, one that's satisfying to the child, something she wants to do, but also something she's forced to do.

Sometimes you can take a low-quality activity and make it into high-quality time for everyone. A bath, for example. You can finish a bath in thirty-seven seconds or you can stretch it out, let your baby play around with a duck, splash to her heart's content and make a joyful mess. (One of the reasons, by the way, that she will love her bath is because it re-creates the comfort, warmth, and ambiance of floating in the amniotic fluid, thought to be the most comfortable position possible for a human being, where all its cares, needs, and wants are taken care of automatically.)

Meals may also be elevated to high-quality time. Not if you feed perfunctorily, shoving a breast or bottle into the baby's mouth, giving the baby three minutes, and then plunking it back down into the crib. Then you have a low-quality experience. A necessary activity has been forced upon the child.

On the other hand, feeding can be a delight for both of you. The baby can kind of rest and cuddle up against you with breast or bottle, and you can both share and enjoy a lovely physical sensation.

Unfortunately, it's easy to be perfunctory, impatient, and anxious with bottles, and if such feeding is chronic that can lead to problems. The frustration babies can suffer in that situation leads to a condition called "failure to thrive," in which the child is a poor feeder, becomes lethargic, loses weight, appears chronically ill for no known organic reason.

You should simply try to relax and enjoy feeding times, making them something positive and high-quality for both of you. Usually, fathers have to be reminded of this before they realize that feeding the baby is done not merely to keep the child alive, that it can be a special experience for him and the child.

YOUR CHILD'S RATE OF DEVELOPMENT

Jessica is thirteen months old and isn't walking. Tony, who lives next door, started to walk at nine months, which threw Jessica's mother into a terrible state. She wants to know if Jessica is retarded.

After carefully examining Jessica, I tell her mother absolutely not. Jessica is perfectly healthy, not suffering from any developmental problems. I also try to explain to her, as I do with so many parents like her, that the developmental tables often found in books and magazines are not simple measuring sticks.

Jessica, like every child, will mature at her own speed. Her language will develop on one line, her muscular development on another line. All of which can be faster or slower than Tony from next door.

As I explained to Jessica's mother, just because one child walks faster than another doesn't mean that that child is any smarter, or that her Jessica is in any way retarded. Intellectual development is on a completely different line of development within the brain.

Happily, children are unique. They develop according to their own schedules, and although you can say in a general way that there is a correlation between walking and talking and the development of intelligence, you must understand that they are broad landmarks.

Pediatricians do use screening devices to pick up the retarded child by certain of the developmental landmarks, but the landmarks they gauge are related to motor development in the grossly impaired child.

That's different from an anxious parent projecting her ambitions on her little girl, measuring how bright the child is by how early she sits or smiles, how early she crawls, how early she walks. Will it make you feel terrific and proud if your child develops ahead of her playmates? Sure—why not? But don't mistake it for something else. It is not a sign of genius.

Earlier, I spoke of the widespread need I encounter among parents to make geniuses of their children. Part of that preoccupation is a misuse of developmental tables and a great overemphasis on motor development as a measure of intellectual and emotional development. As I said to Jessica's mother: "Does it make any sense to you that just because Jessica may be a little uncoordinated right now, she's stupid?"

HIGH-QUALITY TIME FOR MOMMY AND DADDY

Give yourself a break. Parenting is hard work, tougher than nearly all parents anticipate. And it's not all joy.

There's a very simple piece of advice I am continually pushing on parents, and the more dedicated they are, the harder I have to push: you should have some high-quality time for yourselves. After the first month or so, when you've made an adjustment to your baby's existence, you and your husband should get out of the house at least once a week for an evening.

To make it more palatable for parents who would feel guilty doing anything for themselves in those first months, I make the point that such a separation, however brief, is also good for their baby. He gets to relate to another person—a baby-sitter, his grandparents, the trusted person you leave him with. And that's good.

Our culture, remember, encourages children to separate from their parents fairly early. At the age of three, children are starting nursery school. That separation will be all the easier for him if he's already been relating to a number of surrogates.

But it is also your well-being I'm thinking of here.

Parents don't' realize what a strain it is to have a baby at the center of their lives, their completely restructured lives, all the time. Gone are the days when the universe consisted of the two of you and your needs, drives, pleasures. Now you are both making sacrifices and compromises, and a very natural resentment can start growing in you both.

Parenting is hard work, and you get resentful of it. Certainly, there are enormous pleasures, but there is also drudgery, cleaning up after baby, changing a million smelly diapers, coping with vomiting, adjusting to the loss of sleep. The effect is cumulative during the first year, and with it comes an increasing amount of unconscious resentment. The resentment leads to guilt over knowing that there are times when you really don't like your baby.

I explain to an awful lot of parents that such feelings are perfectly normal. After all, if you've got your own cold, or just had a great disappointment at work, and your baby is being as demanding and noisy as ever, why shouldn't you feel as if you could throttle the child?

All parents go through a period in the first six months when they think that maybe they've bitten off more than they can chew. Physically, emotionally, financially, the burdens seems intolerable. It's very helpful at this time if you can compare nightmares with other couples and see that you are not alone in the world. Fortunately, this point usually coincides with the period during which the little creature is beginning to turn into a little person, somewhere around eight or nine months.

But you can begin to see how something that you took so for granted—a night out for the two of you—can become an important refuge and a restorative during this time. I have seen parents who for one reason or another were not able to give themselves even a few days a month, and toward the end of the first year, when their baby was getting increasingly responsive to them, increasingly enjoyable, they were worn out. They were frazzled, guilty, resentful, and thought of themselves as bad parents. It took them a year to shake the effects of that first grinding stretch.

VACATIONS WITHOUT BABY

Evenings out are one thing. Extended periods away from your child at this stage in his life are something else. Beyond a possible weekend escape, vacations without your baby during the first fourteen months are not very wise.

First, your baby hasn't yet got any fixed sense of time, and your being away for more than two days could seem like forever to him. Even two days could be disturbing to him.

Further, I've encountered too many parents who aren't comfortable on any extended vacation. They're not sufficiently confident with their surrogate and end up worried and guilty the whole time. What kind of vacation can you have if you're constantly calling home in fear?

Again, I think parental high-quality time is extremely important. But I would start with one night out each week, then maybe the two of you could take a day off together, perhaps build to two days. Do not suddenly disappear from your child's presence and live for a week or two in Paris or the Swiss Alps during this first stage of his life.

BUSINESS TRIPS

Obviously, if you can cut down on these absences as well, life will be less stressful for you and your baby.

If you and your husband are both working, try to

schedule your business trips so that one of you is always home. That will greatly relieve the anxiety of the traveling parent, especially during the first months. It takes at least six months to feel comfortable and trustful with your surrogate, so only if one of you is home will the other feel somewhat reassured that your baby is being properly taken care of.

From the child's point of view, before eight months, if one of you must be away, it isn't going to make a great difference, assuming the other is available and the child has a caregiver he's somewhat attached to.

From about nine months to a year, he'll be able to distinguish between you and anyone else taking care of him, and he'll make more of a fuss over the separation. Which, of course, will mean more guilt for you. But there is absolutely no data that indicates that your baby will be harmed by this kind of brief separation.

In other words, this situation is tougher on the parents than the child. With one of you around, as well as the surrogate, by now familiar to the baby, he still has the basic elements of a secure environment.

You, on the other hand, are not only anxious about your baby's well-being, you are terribly guilty. You are abandoning your baby, some inner voice tells you, in the pursuit of your own selfish goals. It is one of the toughest guilt burdens of a working mother.

YOUR SEPARATION ANXIETY

Earlier in this chapter, I spoke of separation anxiety and of ways your child will practice reassuring herself that you are there, that you will not abandon her.

Parents have their own forms of separation anxiety, though usually they can cope, and, for example, finally leave their children and let them walk down the hall to the nursery school classroom.

However, I receive a large number of referrals from pediatricians of parents who cannot make any break.

They sit for months at home, hovering over their infants. Their anxiety over separation feeds their child's anxiety, and that child will get very intractable and difficult unless a parent is close to her.

I saw one mother who was extremely ambivalent about having had her child. She was guilt-ridden over her negative feelings about the baby, and as I've frequently seen in such a situation, she couldn't accept or deal with her negative feelings. So instead of coming to terms with the fact that the baby was an imposition, she harbored guilt. Anytime she left the baby, she felt angry and resentful about having had the baby. Indeed, she thought at such times that she didn't want to return to her baby. But she couldn't handle such thoughts, so instead she never left the baby at all.

I see another side of this ambivalence and fear and guilt in mothers who take their children everywhere. It doesn't matter how inappropriate the outing might be; they take them to parties, to their business, everywhere. Again, if they don't ever leave their babies, they won't have to face those deeply disturbing feelings of anger, resentment, and the fear that what they really want is to leave their babies altogether.

A FATHER'S AMBIVALENCE

With fathers who have mixed or even completely negative feelings about having a baby in their lives, I've seen another pattern. They "disappear," and they do it in a way that our culture makes very easy for them: they throw themselves into their jobs, working later and harder, from eight in the morning until nine at night, proclaiming all the while that they must work such long hours because now the family has such heavy extra expenses.

I recall two cases where the fathers didn't want to have the babies. When the children arrived, they both assumed the work dodge as a way of leaving the unwanted scene and manifesting their anger. They were abandoning their wives, yet on the surface they appeared to be responsible providers. In both cases, not surprisingly, they declared that they couldn't afford any surrogate help, thereby really trapping their wives with their babies.

In one of those cases, the father acted with some conscious awareness of what he was doing. His position was that he had not wanted a baby and had made himself completely clear to his wife. If that was the life she wanted, she could have it—without him. He pushed his marriage into divorce.

The other man was not aware of his feelings. He suppressed them, covered them under the rationalization of the anxious father trying to earn more than ever.

I was able to sit down with him and his wife and get him to see what had actually happened. "Your wife is dropping dead from exhaustion," I told him. "And she is a very bright woman who wants to be able to go back to her work too." With some therapy, they were able to save themselves and their marriage.

ANXIETY BREEDS ANXIETY

Baby Carl was irritable, continually crying, refusing to eat. His parents brought him to the hospital, confused and scared.

Was this a colicky baby, born difficult? Or was there something about the parents and the atmosphere they created for him that caused him to be a "failure to thrive" child?

We handled Carl as we usually treat babies showing these symptoms: separated him from his parents. Sure enough, within two days he was eating and the nurses were having no problems dealing with him. Within a week he was gaining weight.

Clearly, there were psychosocial problems affecting

him in his home. And on interviewing his mother, I found an extremely anxious woman.

Carl, like any normal baby, was very sensitive to his environment. He picked up on his mother's anxieties and they bred a kind of anxiety in him.

This is not always the case. Sometimes the irritability in a baby, as I previously noted, can be inborn. In that situation, if the parents are unable to handle that difficult disposition, their own tenseness, unfortunately, will feed and nurture it.

THE BEGINNINGS OF DISCIPLINE

As we approach the end of this Age of Dependency, the major biologic change in your child I mentioned earlier occurs. He is able to walk.

With that, he is no longer totally dependent on you. He can locomote, career and crash around on his own. And that new power will inspire him to explore the universe as he never did before (which we'll examine in the next chapter, "The Age of Exploration").

There have been times during the first fourteen months when you certainly said no to him. You have pulled things out of his mouth, restrained him from crawling off a porch, kept him from touching a hot stove.

But with walking the troubles he can heave himself into multiply, and so must your efforts at discipline.

When parents come to me, troubled by what they call "disciplinary problems" with their infants, I have to find out what they mean. Usually, they feel their child is deliberately breaking rules, and they want to put a stop to it early.

I point out to them that no infant under the age of twelve to fourteen months consciously breaks any rules, because children of that age don't have enough of a conscious mind to know what the rules are.

After all, your child might simply be exploring, taking advantage of this great new power to walk that he has. He might be responding to a strong pleasure drive, or even consciously pushing his luck, wanting to go somewhere or do something even though he understands he ought not to.

For his safety and a healthy environment—and your sanity and future relationship with him—discipline is important.

I view the problem on three levels: limit setting, discipline, and punishment.

Limit setting comes first in life and it means saying no. As I've noted, you've undoubtedly been doing this more and more as this first stage evolved. You've pointed out places that are out of bounds, things that are not to be picked up, even attitudes that you want to discourage. As we'll see in the next chapter, when we discuss exploration at length, there are ways to say no and be effective about it; screaming and giving lectures are not among them.

Discipline is a response to the conscious breaking of rules, and it comes later in the next stage. It is depriving your child of something he values because he did break a rule. Bear in mind that in order for discipline to be effective your child must have developed enough so that he can really understand what you're saying. If you tell him not to touch anything in the medicine cabinet, he must be able to comprehend what the medicine cabinet is and what your prohibition is. If he consciously understands and then breaks your rule, discipline makes sense.

The process also assumes that your child will be old enough to have objects in his life that truly matter to him. Otherwise, you've got nothing meaningful to deprive him of.

Punishment is a negative reinforcement of a crime. Never do this again, it says, or you'll be hurt again. It can mean being confined to a room or physically hurt, and that should be so rare that it happens about once a year.

Basically, a punishment should only be inflicted when your child breaks the rules in such a serious way that he is endangering himself or someone else.

During the first six years, there are three general categories of crime requiring punishment.

1. When he does something dangerous such as standing in a window or running out into traffic. One mother told me that her three-year-old daughter had run off into traffic, and that she, the mother, actually scared herself by sweeping the child off the street, rushing back to the sidewalk, and rather uncontrollably whacking the child right across the bottom. It was the only time she had ever struck the girl, and the violence of the whole scene disturbed her. But in fact, that was the time for a spanking.

When you do resort to physical punishment, don't slap your child across the face. Hospital emergency rooms regularly treat children with terrible eye injuries from even a light slap. Whomps on the fanny will serve the purpose and not lead to accidental injuries.

2. When he abuses you or someone else physically, bites you or his little sister.

3. When he lies overtly, which won't happen much before six years or older, because he won't have the tools for it.

More on this important subject to come in Chapter 3.

TRAUMATIZING YOUR CHILD

"I did it to the child," the woman told me. "I made him crazy and neurotic, and now he can't get along with other children and won't do his work in school. His life is a mess, and it's barely started."

That kind of guilt and fatalism is commonly heard in my office, and is greatly misplaced. Yet, when you found out you were pregnant and asked yourself if you could be a good parent, you were not thinking of feeding and providing alone. A parent's deeper concern is: Will I shape a psychologically healthy child? Or will I create an unbalanced person who might do God knows what damage to himself and others?

There are great misconceptions at work here. The first is the theory of the single psychological trauma, which says that you can do something to your child once and destroy him forever. I often heard this connected with toilet training. "I started training him too early. He really wasn't ready for it, but I forced him, and that must have done it. Completely traumatized him."

What these distressed parents don't understand is that a trauma to the psyche must be chronic and it must be severe. In other words, you have to be really dedicated to a damaging pattern of behavior in order for it to afflict your child. Losing your temper as your child sits on the potty will not do it. Nor will having a slimy, screaming wrestling match with your daughter to keep her from throwing food.

It is not these single events, as searing as they might seem at the moment, that warp a child's personality. You can certainly affect your child during the toilet training period or over the issue of food, but you must do it in a chronic, harsh, repeated pattern.

Chronic physical or sexual abuse, for example, will scar your child. Chronic disruption of the family, continual fighting between you and your husband, yelling and beating each other, can do it. So can chronic emotional abuse of the child—repeated rejection, ridicule, hostility. But those are clearly different matters from the occasional scene.

The single psychological trauma theory seems to me a misunderstanding of Freud. He did have such a theory in connection with an early explanation of phobias: a man walked under a window, got hit with a pot of flowers, and then developed a fear of going into the street.

But that was only a partial explanation of phobias, and Freud discarded it quickly because it simply did not stand up to observed data.

Yet, from parents who come to me and from what I read in the popular press, I see that the misconception is widely accepted: one critical event equals one psychological scar.

You as a parent do not have to worry that any lapse or slip is going to ruin your infant. In fact, increasingly over the last fifteen years or so, the evidence indicates that you might have much more to do with bringing out the best in your child than with being the root cause for any mental illness or disturbance in his functioning later in life.

Increasingly, it is clear that parenting is only one of three shaping powers when it comes to personality formation and disturbance. The other two powers in this equation are life experience and biochemical or genetic factors, and you might weigh them equally.

By life experience I mean the way, for example, your child experiences the arrival of a sibling. Some children handle it very well, some poorly. How they respond to it and interpret it is not merely a function of the actions of their parents but is also a function of their own temperament.

How your child experiences the limits you place on him is an important phase of discipline that we'll discuss in the next chapter. For some children it is an assault, and they get furious. Such children frequently end up in my office. Other children accept it easily. They let their parents set limits for them, seem to recognize that limit setting is a function of parents, and they accommodate it.

I spoke of genetic vulnerabilities earlier in this chapter. The last fifteen to twenty years have proved to researchers that nature plays a major role in the development of severe personality disturbances. When we saw that we could use chemical management in mental illness—when we could use phenothiazines to chemically affect schizophrenia, for example—we knew that there was something going on inside that was not purely environmental, that was not the result of traumatic confrontations with parents during the early formative years.

Parenting has nothing to do with such disturbances, which in a way should be a relief. It can also be upsetting because many people cannot accept the possibility that something so important is out of their control, that their child's mental health is to some degree predestined.

Yet what we have operating on your child's personality is a very complex amalgam, an interaction of heredity, of the events of life, of you—but not of you alone.

One of the errors of early psychologists was focusing only on parents to explain the development of human personality. It was, again, a misinterpretation of Freud. He actually never said, "It's all parents." People overlook the fact that Freud was a neurophysiologist who made clear statements that the root cause of most neurosis was to be found in the genes. But he didn't have the tools of chemistry, the neurophysiological tools to go further in that direction. Only in recent years have we been able to do that, to examine genetic elements, to study the inheritance of temperament.

Early psychologists also tended to perceive the personality as completely cast during the first five years of life. Today, it seems clear that the personality in general is much more plastic than we used to think.

It still appears that the essential personality is formed during the first five years, but many people can change after that time, reshaped by life experiences or by therapy. We now know that many changes take place later in life, and we're just beginning to appreciate how complicated they are. We see from Piaget's work, for example, that there are new levels of abstract thinking that develop as late as age fifteen or sixteen. The biology of human beings is evolving up to the late teens and early twenties, probably indicating that the brain is changing in subtle ways we don't fully appreciate yet. Elderly people are capable of great change.

All of which should reassure you further. When you inflict what you are sure is a terrible trauma, you are in all likelihood being much too hard on yourself. Your child will not be scarred forever. You're going to have good days and bad days with your child, and you're going to make lots of mistakes. But that little creature has the capacity to accept lots of mistakes. What it cannot stand, however, without having a psychological toll, is continuous punishment in the broadest sense over long periods of time.

3

The Age of
Exploration

(14 to 30 months)

You are going to hear the sound of your own voice a great deal during this stage, and it will be saying, "No, no. That is a no-no."

Or, "Don't do that. . . . Sweetheart, please don't do that."

Or, "Stop. Do not touch that."

Or, "Lord, will you please give me a break?"

This is a time of conflict, inevitable conflict. Fairly quickly, you will understand why this period is called "the terrible twos."

To start with, your child can now walk. His power to locomote is absolutely exhilarating to him, and he will go everywhere and get into everything. Mobility is his latest pleasure, and as you will recall from the last chapter, he is still a creature strongly in tune with his pleasure principle.

Obviously, although this makes for great excitement for both of you, it can also create all kinds of new and serious problems.

Unintentionally, he can now be destructive. He can push a stack of china dishes off a shelf so they end up on the floor in a pile of broken pieces.

Worse, he can get under the sink and, while investigating all those fascinating cans, boxes, and bottles stored there, help himself to a drink of Lysol or lye and poison himself (this is, in fact, one of the most common causes of emergency room visits for children of this age).

You must prevent that or anything like it from happening, and that means you must limit his explorations to a certain degree. Some of your precautions can be "baby-proofing" your home: move the china up to a shelf he can't reach, put a lock on the cabinet under the sink, stick plastic covers into the open electric outlets around the house so he can't stick his fingers, wet from his mouth, into them.

But much of your controlling will be verbal, and it will be frequent. As I said, you will hear yourself delivering a lot of "No, no." And of course, as you do, you are in conflict to some degree with your child's pursuit of pleasure.

He in turn is beginning to relate to you in a new way. You are now for him an authority figure, a loving authority figure, it is hoped, but one nonetheless. During this period he will learn to relate to authority figures, a meaningful psychological and cultural condition that he will be coping with throughout his life.

There is something of a logical paradox in our culture when it comes to the individual and authority, and we start to see it mirrored in your child's struggles here. Our society rewards the person who relates well to authority—the white-collar worker, for example, who postpones gratification, adheres to rules and regulations, possesses certain high-level skills that he can use in working with others. At the same time, we prize individuality, being independent, being your own boss, reaching for the moon.

There's a balance between the two, between good relations with authority and autonomy, which evolves in a healthy individual. Now we see your child in an early confrontation with this. It is hoped that you will create for him an environment in which he can grow as an individual but also be willing to give up freedom under certain circumstances.

This is a period, as Erik Erikson said, when your child is defining for himself his levels of autonomy. The way he relates to authority figures will certainly be significantly determined during this stage.

In this important process of juggling, you can see where that basic trust I spoke of in the last chapter is so meaningful. Without it, it's tough to get your child to give up his pleasure principle. Why not put your head in the toilet bowl, except that Mommy says don't do it? Why not put your finger into the socket and get the pleasure you think it might hold, except that Mommy says it's a no-no?

Through all of this, life will be easier if you can remember once again that your child has nothing in mind except pleasure and seeing what's going to happen. He has no idea of hurting himself or anybody else, or of breaking anything. He is not deliberately attempting to disobey you or in any way trying to make life difficult for you. He is merely following that drive to explore everything.

Your saying no, or physically carrying him away from something, will be the first overt conflict in his life. The basic trust that has evolved between you two will, as I said, help you both work it out. In the ideal world, children would abandon their pursuit of pleasure for love alone. But in our real world, as we'll see later in this chapter, there might well have to be some kind of payoff for him. In his mind at times he'll be saying, "Well, if I'm going to stop playing in the toilet, what's in it for me?" In other words, he's looking for a reward, and with a couple of cautions, I have no problem with payoffs or rewards. It's no crime to give him a cookie or some ice cream so long as limits are observed.

However, don't be too quick with that capitalistic reward. It might be the simplest technique for you, but it's not necessarily the best in the long run. If love alone doesn't move him, try the gold star system that we discuss on page 86 first. He'll learn more from that.

Some of the conflict of this stage, by the way, will be diminished if you followed my advice during the first stage of your child's life and, without meaning to sound cruel, let him taste a bit of frustration. You might recall that I suggested that you try not to leap every time he gave a cry from his crib; that he might well, from six months on, handle a bit of delay and develop a slight frustration tolerance. That tolerance can make it easier for him now, when he is confronted with countless situations where he will not get everything he wants.

LIMIT SETTING

One of your major tasks during this period will be setting limits for your child. How far can he go? How much can he do? What behavior is acceptable and what is not?

There was a time not so long ago when it was fashionable to do as little limit setting as possible. That was a mistake, I think. Rather, the challenge should be to understand what limits ought to be set, how to set them and make them stick, and how to sort them out for your child so that he grasps which are the most important ones, what your hierarchy is among them.

To minimize limit setting is to ignore an important reality of our society (as well as to make life close to intolerable for yourself). It goes back to relating to authority. In our society, to get along well, you have to be accepting of the authority figure. That doesn't mean regimentation—no autonomy or individuality.

Of course, toilet training, which usually begins at between eighteen and twenty-four months, remains a common problem area. From your point of view, what you are doing is advancing your child one great step into civilized society. For you it's pretty clear and automatic. After all, no one can really go through life wearing diapers.

However, your two-year-old doesn't know about civilized society. From his point of view, you are asking him to give up a major pleasure, the pleasure of simply defecating whenever he pleases. You are asking him to abandon that for the control of the potty. To him, the potty is a kind of scary thing in and of itself. He sees it as something he could fall into. It also makes a very loud noise. You can begin to imagine the potential contest of wills that can develop over this, and we'll consider it later in this chapter.

NEGATIVISM AND TEMPER TANTRUMS

The two most common problems parents of normal children come to me with during this period are negativism—when the child says no to everything—and temper tantrums.

As for negativism, children will at first test any and all limits, even the dangerous ones. If you have been chronically giving in to them, their direct resistance will build and all training will be very difficult.

Temper tantrums are a form of physical protest, sometimes due to temperament and sometimes due to too-stringent limits on the child's behavior. If the parents become too responsive to the temper tantrums, they can unknowingly encourage that very behavior.

In general, no matter how well behaved your child is, it's a good idea to expect one major temper tantrum during this stage. He is going to test the system before he accepts the idea that no is really no.

Very often I find that parents haven't established priorities within the limits they've set on the child's activities. Everything is no. That's all the child hears. He has no autonomy at all.

That won't work. Not only should you have a hierarchy of limits, but your rules, to be effective, should be conveyed to your child by certain tones of voice and facial expressions.

For a child from fourteen to twenty months old, simply saying no or yelling at him for any length of time without conveying displeasure in your face probably won't be picked up by him as a communication. Very often, a no has to be accompanied by a mean look, an angry face. Mothers frequently tell me they scream all day at their children, only to have their husbands come home and, whammo, merely look at the uncontrollable monster and the creature suddenly behaves.

The point is that nonverbal, physical communication is terribly important. And by "physical" I definitely do not mean slapping or shaking a child. I do not believe in corporal punishment at this age. Nonverbal means an angry look, which apparently Daddy delivers more readily and naturally than Mommy.

Many of the problems I encounter come from children who don't know what behavior is appropriate. Their parents do not set clear limits or clearly communicate the rules. Or they set such broad limits, often unconsciously, that the child is frustrated by finding most of her behavior under attack.

One anxious mother who came to me set her limits in a rather literal way and it was futile. She had great difficulty with a four-year-old who was hyperactive and suffered a learning disability. Also, she and her husband were both rather obsessive about cleanliness.

So whenever her normal younger son, age two, wanted to do anything at all messy, as two-year-olds love to do, she popped him into the empty bathtub. There he was supposed to sit and play with his finger paints, confining his mess.

Of course, at two a child is going through separation and individuation and is "practicing," as we discussed in the last chapter. So three minutes after being dumped into the tub, the little boy was out, carrying his messy paints, looking around the house for his mother, check-

ing on her. It was hopeless. Limit setting does not mean
confining a child to a bathtub. Children must have some
autonomy, some freedom to explore.

There were a number of ways the mother might have
handled this problem to the satisfaction of everybody.
It's true that two-year-olds are capable of remarkable
messes, and who wants to live with that all over the
house? But the mother might have simply spread newspapers in the child's room when he wanted to paint. Or
covered a corner of his room with a sheet of linoleum,
which is easy to clean. Maybe even given the little boy
only crayons until he was able to control his mess better. She also could have let him know by her expression
and tone of voice that it was important that he do what
she told him—that he only paint on the linoleum, for
example.

If you have in your own mind the things the child
ought not to do, and which are most important among
them, then you should let him know. Your no's should
be clear, unequivocal, loud, and weighted by voice and
facial expression according to their rating on your list
of what matters most.

So, stern disapproval would go with any dangerous
activity, such as playing around with an electric outlet
or climbing onto a windowsill.

A milder no would be suitable if he gets in the way
as you're carrying hot food across the room. That could
be potentially dangerous to both of you, but it is certainly not life threatening. Climbing on a living room
chair he's not supposed to be on merits a milder no.

Your child will begin to discriminate.

While you're establishing these limits, you should arrange your house so your child can explore it with few
constraints. As I mentioned, move all dangerous sub-
stances out of his reach: no cleaning fluids left under
the sink, no drugs on a low shelf in a medicine cabinet;
nothing the child can mistake for food should be reach-
able. Move the breakables. Install window guards. All

of this will not only protect your child's life, but it will eliminate countless screaming battles between the two of you.

You'll also have to establish limits for him outside the house, especially in the place where most two-year-olds are introduced to social life—the supermarket.

Every two-year-old is going to want to pull things off the shelves, and you can greet that with a clear no but without any fierce look. A moderate no, in other words, conveying the idea that pulling a cereal box off a shelf is not as serious as climbing onto a windowsill at home but is still not acceptable behavior.

Using these nuances in your limit setting repertoire, and helping your child to grasp them, will result in a more responsive child.

It could also cut down on the chances of temper tantrums, though, as I said, at this stage you should expect a severe temper tantrum now and then.

They come in two basic forms: In the first, your child lies on the floor, kicking and screaming and generally carrying on. The second is a rarer and more terrifying variety: breath holding. Children who have very intense temperaments will have breath-holding spells.

Deal with both in the same way. Ignore them. Understand that ignoring your child is the ultimate rejection. You should communicate to him strongly with words and looks that you are not going to accommodate him, you are not going to respond to him until he behaves in a more appropriate way.

The point is not to reward him either way. Though in your frustration you might not think so, hitting a child under those circumstances is actually a kind of negative reinforcement, and that is more meaningful to him than ignoring him. But "turning away," as it's called, is a treatment that is extremely painful to him and in my view you should use it to respond to only the most disapproved-of behavior, as with tantrums. Turning away is an effective technique. Chances are your child will stop throwing tantrums because he will see it's useless, it gets no response from you.

If your child throws his fit in a public place, I would consider an exception to the "rejection" treatment. As a last resort—after trying to reason, cajole, threaten—I would consider physical intervention. If you can, lift him up and carry him away to a more private area. If this is impossible, then a slap on the buttocks might work. Assuming you have not hit him before, if you surprise him with such a slap you might successfully cut the temper tantrum in midstream and the two of you can leave the store and retreat from a possibly embarrassing and difficult situation.

The effectiveness of your surprise attack depends on its being a real surprise. Repeated slapping and hitting of a child will make one more crack meaningless. And, as I've noted, that's the least effective thing you can do for temper tantrums, the worst negative reinforcement of the act.

As you might realize, the desperate slap might become necessary because your other usual alternatives are not available. You can't very well walk away and leave him all alone in the middle of a large supermarket. You don't have any room you can send him to, or even one that you can walk into yourself.

If you do spank him, don't feel too terrible about it. A single slap on the fanny does not make you an ogre of a parent.

You should expect that every once in a while during this period, as much as you love your child, he is going to drive you to complete distraction and you are going to lose your temper and your cool. The terrible twos are guaranteed to do that. Absolutely normal on your part, especially when you're juggling a dozen bags, in addition to your child, in a crowded store.

Although much of your parenting at this time will necessarily be concerned with limit setting and expressing a symphony of disapprovals, you should also be expressing approval to your child.

Positive reinforcement is the other side of the hierarchy of no's and your child needs it.

Give your child plenty of approval for appropriate behavior. And when you have a successful no, give a hug, a kiss, to let your child know you're pleased. At this age, your child needs to have the feeling that he's still wanted and loved. You don't want him to feel that he is doing only bad, "no-no" things.

In addition to that kind of affectionate approval, your child will also need you and that high-quality playtime we've discussed, lots of smearing finger paints together, rolling balls, beating on pots and pans. (Children at this age have a drive for sensory stimulation, and making that noise gives them tremendous pleasure.)

You will finally know that you've connected, that your child really does understand the word "no" when he starts what we call "identification with the aggressor." It's the first sign of the primitive Superego, or primitive conscience.

He will start to say no to you, sometimes over and over. And he will begin saying it to some "transitional object": his teddy bear, blanket, something he clings to when he's practicing separation, such as when you take him from your home to stay at Grandma's.

So after you tell him he may not have a cookie, you will see him some while later saying to his teddy bear, "No, no, no, no. No cookie."

When you see that kind of imitating, you can feel confident that he understands, at long last, that no is giving up a pleasure, at least temporarily, in order to keep your love and acceptance.

Now let's consider some of these developments in greater detail.

THE ANAL STRUGGLE

The Age of Exploration is a period, as I noted, that is especially characterized by your child's first struggles and conflicts over limits.

There is no clearer model of this than the anal struggle between you and her, a conflict that was particularly meaningful to Freud.

What's happening is that you are asking, or telling, your child to postpone the pleasure of doing whatever she wants to do whenever she feels like it. "Don't poop in your diaper," you tell her. "In fact, you're getting to be such a big girl, you don't even have to wear a diaper anymore. But when I take your diaper off, don't go on the floor. Tell Mommy when you want to go and Mommy will put you on the potty and you'll go to the bathroom like a big girl, just like Mommy does."

You draw on the basic trust between you two, you cajole, you reward. But she knows the game is changing. There are new rules. Depending on the personalities of parents and child, this struggle can be a fierce clash of wills or it can be traversed without enormous strain.

In Freud's time, the struggle was traditionally a terrible one. Toilet training often started at a premature age, around ten to twelve months, and the parent essentially told the child, Do what I say or else. Embodied in this approach was the concept that the child should yield to the power of authority.

One of the reasons we place less emphasis on the meaning of the anal conflict today is that, in general, our way of raising children has changed.

We expect some adherence to authority, but we also allow a certain amount of autonomy. We cut the chances for profound anal struggle. To begin with, it is generally accepted practice not to try toilet training before eighteen to nineteen months. Before then, quite simply, no child has very good sphincter control.

Also, I think we're much more relaxed about succeeding. If you try toilet training and it simply isn't working, stop for six weeks, then try again. Eventually it will happen, allowing for occasional accidents.

Some parents receive unexpected assistance from preschools. Of course, not all children start school or prenursery at three, but if you're planning on doing that with your child, and she's three and still not completely trained, odds are she'll quickly finish the job herself. One of her first encounters with peer pressure will do it. She'll realize that all her classmates are going to the potty, and she'll decide the time has come for her as well.

I don't recommend deliberately leaving the job of toilet training to the likely effect of this peer pressure, but knowing about it might help you relax if your child is having some trouble around the potty and her first day of preschool is approaching.

What Freud also saw in this process was that excretory functions begin to take on a new meaning for the child. They get tied up with the postponement of pleasure, and also with a kind of infantile form of sexuality, the pleasure the child experiences when she can finally let go.

Indeed, when you think about it, Freud was touching on something any adult can relate to. Not to be too crass, but have you ever gone for hours without relieving yourself? Driving through the countryside in a rainstorm, with no service station open, no restaurant for miles and miles? And finally, thank heaven, a diner, and you bolt for the bathroom? Leave your husband and child in the car to cope for themselves and make a run for it? To be honest about it, isn't there a certain amount of sexual pleasure in relieving yourself after all that denial and postponement?

Freud thought that this pleasure for the child, the denial of it, and the struggle over who would control her physical functions brought a new awareness to her of her excretory apparatus. The whole toilet training process caused her to focus much more on her sexual parts and to become aware that there are differences between the sexes when it comes to going to the bathroom.

She may have possessed some vague sense before this that Daddy has a penis and Mommy does not, she has a vagina; that Daddy urinates standing up and Mommy sits down. Now, however, she becomes aware of these differences between the sexes right at a time when she is developing a much keener sense of her own sexual identity.

To Freud and his followers, a child's basic sexual or gender identity is established at this time, between the ages of two and three. This is when a child's innate psychological sexual identity takes hold. In a superficial way, this is when a girl knows she is a girl and different from a boy, when she becomes vaguely aware that her genital organs look different from those of a boy, even if she has absolutely no idea of the uses of the two parts in the process of reproduction.

Partly as a result of all this churning in your child's mind, you might find her especially curious about the bathroom habits of you and your husband. You might also find her talking a lot about her own private parts, declaring to you and the world that she has them, and that her father has a penis, or that her brother or Johnny next door has one.

It can be a little unnerving, suddenly having this two-foot-tall sexologist in your house, but it's all perfectly normal, her innocent way of affirming her identity as a woman. It is the beginning of that terribly important development I discussed earlier, establishing gender identity, which later on in life allows our species to survive and grow.

Freud basically perceived the child as frequently being quite torn about submitting to toilet training. She is confronted with a yes/no, good/bad conflict, and she says, I don't want to change because peeing whenever

I feel like it gives me pleasure. On the other hand, if I don't give in, Mommy won't love me.

Then the child says it's her parent, usually Mommy, who's the bad one in this drama. She's awful and I hate her, is the child's new feeling. But she also retains feelings of love and dependency for Mommy. From that ambivalence comes an inner sense of primitive guilt in the child.

How she deals with this disturbing guilt and a number of other unpleasant feelings around the age of twenty-four months leads us to the extremely complex area of defense mechanisms, or coping mechanisms.

Let me try to sketch some of this out.

Basically, these mechanisms are ways your baby develops to deal with anything that's unpleasant.

If we go back a bit to her early months, she seems to have one primary method of coping and that is denial. If she's hungry and can't satisfy that need, she might cry and kick a bit, but finally she will deny that unpleasant feeling by going to sleep.

Later on in life we'll see a different use of coping with a more abstract feeling that disturbs her. Around three, she might know the feeling of helplessness. So, she starts playing and invokes fantasy. Suddenly, she is Wonder Woman, racing about the house, able to solve all your earthly problems. Through her play, she is replacing her helpless reality. This is called "reaction formation," a more subtle method of coping.

Quite early—say, around twelve months—she might well have to confront a number of unpleasant, unwanted feelings, ideas, and thoughts. To take a stark example, let's say you have another child. What she perceives is that a little brother has invaded her world. What she wants to do to that creature who has taken away a certain amount of your time and affection is, quite simply, to kill it.

Somehow she knows she can't do that and that the very idea is really bad. A new mechanism then seems to come into play: "repression." Repression makes that bad idea and the bad feelings that come with it all go away. All of that ugly mess is forced into the Unconscious, or at least that's the theory.

But repression does not seem to be enough. There still seem to be nasty kinds of feelings toward that tiny brother. The conscious part of the mind, the Ego, must have other ways to take that destructive energy and do something with it. So new coping mechanisms evolve.

We see this rather clearly around the anal conflict, where she is dealing with the good/bad dilemma. She is also dealing with criticism, which is unpleasant for her.

Or, around that same age, as we noted, she might be encountering criticism in other aspects of limit setting. No, no, no, never put your finger in that socket.

Clearly, she doesn't like the feelings she is left with, so she invokes a kind of denial. "I'm not the little girl who's doing the bad thing." Instead she identifies with the aggressor; she becomes the nasty parent who's telling her she's such a bad little girl. She takes all the angry feelings she feels inside herself and becomes the angry person; she might very well take it all out on her doll. She "displaces" those feelings onto her doll, "projects" the badness on the doll. And the doll becomes the bad person.

"Bad, bad girl," she says to the doll, and whacks it a few times—displacement, projection. She discharges her anger and feels better. A nice way to cope.

This projection will evolve further. One day you may come home and find that she's peed on the floor. You'll ask her, "Why did you do that? You know you're the good girl who pees in the potty." "I didn't do that," she may reply. "Gulliver [the dog] did it." Or, "Baby Boy [her doll] did it."

We adults project when we defensively, sometimes reflexively, tell the boss: "Report? You didn't ask me to do any report. You assigned that to somebody else."

From the confluence of events and feelings of this period, most especially from toilet training, your child begins, according to Freud, an internal struggle over right and wrong.

Freud conceived of a primitive Superego, which represents you, the parent. The Superego says to your child, "This is bad. If you don't do what Mommy or Daddy says, it is bad."

On the other hand, the Id, the unbridled pleasure force, is saying, "Nonsense. Doing what you want—making yourself feel good—is very, very good."

Struggling between the two is her tiny Ego, trying to discern what is really good and what is really bad.

In theory, everything she absorbs—knowledge, information, experience—gets enmeshed in this struggle. Should I? Shouldn't I?

One of the possible effects is "obsessionalism," which is the indecisiveness that goes with ambivalence. The obsessive can't make up her mind, and that's associated with the desire to please the parent versus the desire to please herself.

In later life, this is the person who is constantly worrying and thinking about the alternatives in everything. Everything becomes a problem. Should I buy this dress? Or that one? This one or that one? Maybe I'd better check out all the dresses in the store across the street, and that one down the block, and then come back here and look again.

Obviously, a certain amount of this obsessionalism is a good thing and is perfectly normal. It makes for people who think before they act, and that includes intelligent consumers.

But the true obsessive is holding back on the decision of which dress to buy, retaining control over that decision—and control is very important to obsessives—until that wonderful moment when she decides to let it all go and she buys the dress.

It was in that context that Freud spoke of stinginess as being an anal characteristic.

The term "obsessive compulsive" is probably familiar to you as well. Obsession and compulsion relate. Compulsion deals with the actions of the obsessive. Compulsivity is the behavior pattern in which the obsessive person, driven by an unconscious guilt, tries to exorcise badness and reenact goodness by repeating an activity over and over and over again.

Compulsions evolve into rituals. If your child is angry with you, where does the anger go? Perhaps into hitting you—a very typical behavior for a two-year-old. Later, when she's civilized, she'll be able to suppress pleasure and the aggressive impulses as well. But two-year-olds aren't very good at that. Instead, they'll hit—or become oral aggressive and bite.

Around the age of three to four, coping with her anger might lead instead to compulsive acts that involve magical, symbolic thinking. For example, we see a child who begins to hit her desk unconsciously. Hitting the desk discharges the anger, so she won't have to hit Mommy.

I had a case where a boy of about three and a half had been walloping his mother. She finally had enough of it and really started to punish him. Within two months he'd have to go through a ritual of touching every single thing in every room he went into. Then he'd feel okay. It took him half an hour to get from his own room to the front door of the house.

He was driving everyone nuts. Mornings were a special agony. He was supposed to go to nursery school, which was part of the problem. He didn't want to go. He wanted to stay home.

Quite unconsciously, the boy had evolved a kind of perfect solution. He had an unconscious urge to be aggressive to his mother. He couldn't bring his anger to consciousness and, like all of us who are not aware of our anger, he was anxious. He didn't know what it was between him and his mother that was bothering him, but he did know that he wanted to delay or avoid nursery school. By going through his touching ritual he displaced his anger and his desire to hit, and simultaneously made nursery school impossible.

In psychotherapy, the boy showed me rather clearly what was bothering him. He kept choosing a number of lady dolls to play with, and at every session he kept hitting them. It wasn't very difficult to see how he felt about his mother.

In talking with her, I encountered a rigid woman who had strict rules for her son and allowed him almost no autonomy. He really could do nothing on his own, not even get angry at her. She was determined to raise a little gentleman, she told me.

I advised her that she had to allow her son to get angry at her. "If he doesn't like going to school every morning," I said, "which he doesn't, let him tell you and you listen to him. Don't slap him down or punish him, but let him rant about it."

My general rule with her, as with other parents, is to allow your children to ventilate their anger as much as they need to. Let them be angry with you, with school, with the world—real and imaginary. Hear them out.

Then, your understanding with them should be, they have to obey. In other words: Say all you please—and it's okay for you to be angry at me. But once you've had your say, once you've expressed your anger, do what I tell you, even if that means going to the school that you just screamed about.

Are you conning your child? Being devious and cruel? Not at all. Remember, this is not the Supreme Court, where sophisticated and learned argument is being rendered in the name of higher verities and justice. This is your kitchen, where your child, who is not yet equipped for subtle argument, is venting feelings.

Being allowed to complain, knowing that it is okay

to be angry, the process of ventilating, all do wonders (often for adults as well as children).

For example, after I got the compulsive little boy's rigid mother to agree to give him permission to complain, his compulsive behavior diminished and later vanished. It took about three months, but he finally did stop touching everything, and even went to nursery school.

We supplemented that school with a playgroup to give him another physical outlet for his energies. He was a physical boy, built like his father, a large, strong man, and needed an outlet for his energies just as he now had one for his angry feelings.

With therapy, his mother was able to come to grips with some of her own problems and become less rigid. She realized that among other things, she had a fear of men, and one of the ways she dealt with this in terms of her son was to dominate him completely.

BIOLOGY AND LIMIT SETTING

Biology will also affect how your child can respond to your limits.

You should recognize two important conditions to start:

1. A two-year-old has a very short attention span.
2. His memory is not very good.

This means that you have to repeat yourself. Parents frequently complain to me: "I've told that child a hundred times 'No,' but he still does it." That's par. You have to tell them a hundred times because they don't remember.

Also, when you want to establish a limit—no playing with the electric outlet—do it exactly when your child is poking around the outlet. Your caution should accompany his act. Never expect him to associate his act with your admonition if you deliver it more than a minute after it happens.

If you start yelling at him five minutes after he was playing with the outlet, to him you are just a parent screaming for no particular reason at all.

I spoke earlier of ignoring certain behavior, especially tantrums, to enforce your limits. If you literally turn away from your child, he experiences a deep rejection. "I'm not going to talk to you as long as you behave like that," you say, perhaps walking into the next room. He will be shaken by that.

You might leave him alone in the room, or if the offense is severe enough, even send him to his room. This tactic has to be used with care. If you do send him to his room at this age, do not close the door. He might feel so abandoned that it could trigger panic in him. Remember, he's very fragile and vulnerable right now when it comes to separation. As I mentioned earlier, this is the time when he is just beginning to "practice," going for little trips on his own into the other room, coming back to be sure you're still there.

Any threat by you to leave him because he's bad, or actually doing so, can then be an effective way of getting him to understand the limits you are setting. But don't do it in such a way as to frighten him half to death.

Another technique you can apply is the reward, the positive reinforcer, sometimes even called a bribe.

To me it's a bribe when you give your child an excessive reward for some behavior. Life will be simpler if you avoid that.

But a reward, under control, can be very effective in shaping behavior—behavior modification, as it's called—given the nature of two-year-olds.

First of all, they are exceedingly selfish. And they live in a world that is tiny. The world revolves around them, and to give up pleasure in this world is not an easy thing to do.

You do not have to resort to bribes too quickly. Your child will give up a fair amount of pleasure in return for the simplest and perhaps nicest kinds of rewards: for praise from you, for kisses and love. You cannot give them too much of any of those sweet elements.

For tougher problems and more stubborn behavior, supplement your personal loving efforts occasionally with a special reward, say, an apple or a cookie.

If you use that technique, ration the rewards, don't give them out all at once. If you give him a cookie for going to the bathroom once, you'll soon find yourself bribing him with rewards every time he goes.

Behavior therapists have a system I like: the gold star chart.

For repeating a behavior a number of times, your child gets the reward of a gold star. If he collects a certain number of gold stars, usually no more than seven, one a day, he gets a special reward.

The stars can be given for doing something, say, going to the bathroom like a grown-up, or for not doing something, such as not having a temper tantrum for a day. Rewarding him when he doesn't do something will make the behavior go away much faster than punishing him. As he gets older, his rewards can be more elaborate than a special treat, ice cream, or dessert. He might want a goldfish or a particular toy. Fine; if he collects an agreed-upon number of stars, that's what he gets.

Two cautions here:

1. Don't make the process too complicated. If he has to cope with twenty behaviors to earn twenty stars, he'll be overwhelmed.

2. Don't use the star system for everything, only for tough problem behaviors. If it's overused, it'll become ineffective.

Start this system when he's somewhere between two and two and a half, focusing on a single behavior, some one thing you want to encourage—or discourage—the most. Get the idea across that every time he does that one good thing—or doesn't do the bad thing—he'll get a star.

Since he won't have a concept of numbers at that stage, use drawings and pictures of a child doing something.

Then, as you move to phase two, add a second behavior. Now it's going to the bathroom the new way, plus no whining.

Try not to overwhelm him. Use the chart only for behaviors that matter.

WORDS AND LANGUAGE

There are words and there is language. One leads to the other, but they are not the same thing. Your child will have words long before he can use them in a recognizable syntax with grammar.

How all this evolves, how much of it is nature and how much is nurture, is a matter of great controversy these days.

Certainly we know that babies make sounds early in life and that by the time they are fourteen to fifteen months old they are doing a fair amount of "babbling." Babbling is a mixture of sounds, some of which all parents interpret as baby's first words, usually "dada" or "mama."

At about sixteen to eighteen months, your baby is making sounds that resemble real words, though clear, unequivocal words don't usually come along much before twenty months.

Some children speak words earlier. They simply have a facility for it and the muscular development necessary. We never think about it, but a host of muscles are involved in speaking, in the tongue, the throat, the face, the cheeks and nasal muscles. If your child does speak sooner than other children, sooner than the charts indicate, fine, but it doesn't mean you have a genius. His speech is merely developing quickly.

If you and your husband and everyone around your baby are naturally verbal, he might be able to pick up a few more words than a baby in a rather silent household. But it won't make a difference in terms of when he can sequence and grammatically organize words. For that to happen, there has to be, according to one controversial current theory, a biological change in your child's brain.

This school of thought which seems to be gaining prominence, holds that word sequences are laid down in the biology of the organism. Your child will acquire something of a natural grammar. To be sure, this is not English grammar as we know it, but a peculiar primitive grammar that some experts feel is innate. (This is all considerably different from the prevailing theories of some twenty-five to thirty years ago. In those days, the belief was that language was learned, absorbed from the surrounding culture. But the evidence today seems otherwise.)

You'll see that even though you speak good English—and in this context, so does the TV—when your child begins to speak in sequential form (two or three words strung together), he will have a grammar all his own. His words will not be organized in accepted sentence form. "Want ball," he says. You'll also see that he uses nouns before pronouns. Nouns are usually signs, as opposed to symbols. A sign for him is a sound that is associated with a specific, concrete object. A symbol comes later; it is an elaboration of the sign, a mental expansion of its meaning.

So, after you tell him directly and indirectly dozens of times that the dining room table is a "table," he understands. It is for him The Table, perhaps the only one like it he's ever seen. And when he says the word "table," that particular one is in his head.

Sometime later he can recognize that a table is a four-legged piece of furniture with a flat top on which plates and glasses and other things can be placed. Now he has a symbol. But he only reaches that symbol experientially; while growing up he sees a different table in the living room, and another in your bedroom, and then he collects them and can finally define "table" as a broader symbol.

In order to have real language, your child needs grammar, syntax, some symbolic ideas, and at least the beginnings of a variety of words from general categories: verbs, adjectives, adverbs, and so on. That comes in the next period, the Age of Communication, from thirty to forty-eight months.

In the present period, from fourteen to thirty months, he will acquire more and more words and be able to communicate with you more concretely, but he will do it largely in a private, nonverbal fashion. He will read faces and looks; point, drag and pull you; scream; associate one or two words with things.

By the end of this stage, children and parents have a fairly elaborate private language of words, gestures, and codes that outside people don't understand much. After thirty months, in the next period, this develops into something that everyone else comprehends.

You will see that your child understands words better than he can speak them. There is something magical in store for you when this breakthrough in communication begins to happen. When you tell him, "Get the ball," you won't be sure that he understands or will respond. The first time he actually turns around and goes and gets the ball is absolutely startling and wondrous.

How much and how quickly he speaks will depend to some degree on the development and control of the various muscles I mentioned. English is particularly demanding, with complicated speech and syntactical patterns, and it requires your child to move from gross motor coordination to pretty fine motor coordination. There are many sounds, such as "r" and "th," that a child simply can't make.

Some children have such difficulty that by five or six

they still haven't acquired the full range of sounds and they need speech therapy, most commonly for lisping.

In general, when it comes to speech I wouldn't worry unless your child isn't speaking some words by thirty months or if he isn't speaking three-to-four word sentences by thirty-six months. In that case, I'd mention it to the pediatrician at the next checkup.

There are some perfectly normal children who are very bright yet don't seem to say much until they are two. And then they say it all. Sometimes they are slow-to-warm-up children who want to be really sure they have it right before they say it.

If, however, your child makes no sounds at all except for crying by the time he's fifteen-to-sixteen months old, have him checked out. He might have a hearing impairment, which is very tough to pick up in the normal course of checkups during the first year of life.

THE REAL WORLD

TOILET TRAINING WITHOUT TRAUMA

Parents often ask me about the psychological damage they can inflict on their child during the battle of toilet training.

First of all, recall the general rule for inflicting trauma that we considered in Chapter 2. A couple of clashes do not a trauma make. It requires a long, drawn-out, repeated pattern of conflict for months before there is any scarring effect on your child's personality.

The simple way to avoid that with toilet training is to back off, if necessary.

Wait until about eighteen months to start, so she has reasonable sphincter control. Then try it for three or four days. If you're not having any success, and she's giving you a hard time, stop for a while. It's not essential to get this accomplished right away.

It could well be that your anxiety to see her toilet

trained is being communicated to her and making the whole process overcharged. Indeed, I have never seen a case of problem toilet training that has not involved an anxious, very tense, or angry parent. That parent was going to triumph, no matter what.

Or a parent can be so deeply afraid of psychologically damaging her child that, as a result, her very fears become self-fulfilling.

One couple came to me because their three-year-old cried every time they put her on the potty. And they were so afraid of traumatizing her, they immediately pulled her off. As a result, they were in knots and they had a three-year-old who was still in diapers.

There was absolutely nothing they told me that suggested they were truly traumatizing the child. It seemed to me quite simply that their own horror of hearing the little girl cry was keeping them from training the child.

Sometimes the most direct technique is the most effective. "Go home," I told them, "and tell your daughter that she is now three, and for being three she's going to get a reward. She won't have to wear her diaper anymore." Beyond everything else, the child was too big for a diaper and the thing was beginning to chafe her. "Tell her that she is too grown up for a diaper, and of course, now that she doesn't have one, she'll make on the potty, just like grown-ups do."

I suggested they try this bold approach for a week, then give me a call. After four days, the mother called and said "an absolute miracle" had occurred.

Of course, your child could be difficult in her own way. She could have a need to resist you, or she could be a difficult-to-manage or slow-to-warm-up child, which we considered in Chapter 2. With toilet training as with everything else, children with those temperaments require a great deal of patience.

Whatever the reason, if the training process is going badly and your child is full of resistance, declare a four-week moratorium. Let everyone calm down and relax.

If you do that, try not to pass judgment on your child, cursing her as defiant or bad or evil, because that will only subvert the purpose of the moratorium.

During this time, you or your housekeeper should try to watch when your child needs to go and what signals she gives. Then, after the four weeks, make an effort to follow that natural timing pattern and gently place her on a potty seat.

By the way, I prefer potty seats to regular toilets for this process. The potty is something special you've gotten for her, a kind of reward. And it's a great deal less threatening than the toilet. Very often a child can be quite terrified of a toilet. As I noted, to her it's a thing she might fall into, a thing that makes a loud noise as it flushes away something that minutes earlier was a part of her.

Toilet Training Through the Night

Just because you train your child to use the toilet during the day doesn't mean she will be trained for night as well.

She should be gaining nighttime control of her bladder by the age of four. But some people don't gain that control until they are teenagers, and it's a most distressing business. That kind of enuresis is often hereditary. So if your child has trouble with nighttime control, try to remember when you managed it and ask your husband when he gained control.

The problem is found mostly with men, and I've found it's hard to get men to talk about it. They're still embarrassed over wetting their beds as teenagers, and they repress the whole experience because it's so painful.

Children with the problem need motivation to overcome it. Some find it when they go away to camp and face a social situation with other children.

There are treatments for enuresis, but not before a child is about eight. There are also mechanical behavior modifiers such as Wee Wee Stop and Enurtone. Both are pads that complete an electric circuit. When your baby wets the bed, the urine hits the pad and that sets off a bell and a light that are next to the bed. They instantly wake the child, and after lots of nights with this happening, she should wake before she urinates. It's the old Pavlovian method of conditioning the child.

For extreme cases, there is also a prescription medication that's fairly effective, imipramine, which your child takes for a period of months. Discuss its use with your pediatrician.

One other system that sometimes works, though it puts a burden on you, is to wake your child at a certain time each night and lead her to the bathroom. That technique will normally train her, but it does mean you have to get up to make it work.

One technique I don't like is depriving the child of fluids. It might leave her with less liquid in her bladder, but it can also cause her to resent you for depriving her and cause problems between the two of you.

Constipation

Just as it's wise to avoid major battles over toilet training, it's wise not to insist on a pattern of bowel movements.

When I first started practicing, a lot of constipated children were brought to me. There were classical battles going on in those days. Parents insisted their children sit and do it; the children resisted, actually holding on to their feces in defiance.

There was also the widespread idea then that children had to have one or two bowel movements a day. It really had nothing to do with health, but was connected to the compulsivity of the parents.

All of that can be avoided if you are patient and try to fit your toilet training to your child's natural cycle.

TERRIBLE TWOS

They can be tough, from twenty-two to thirty months, shouting their protests: "No, no, no. I won't. . . . Get out. This is my room." But it's natural. It is their struggle for autonomy.

In fact, if you have a child who never protests or argues, look at him closely. Not to alarm you, but an excessively passive child might be anemic or have some other physical ailment that the pediatrician should check out.

How rough this period is depends a great deal on you, your demands on your child, your flexibility.

One couple came to me because they thought their little boy, about twenty-eight months old, was being disrespectful.

Every time they asked him to do something, he told them, "Get out, stupid!" They both were successful businesspeople, and after a while they found this lack of respect hard to tolerate.

But when I looked into things, I found that although he did call them "stupid" every chance he had, he then did what they told him to do.

It seemed to me that the little boy had found a verbal way of dealing with the anger he felt over following an order from an adult. He was actually quite precocious. He had an extensive vocabulary, and his way was to express his negative feelings verbally, then cooperate. That is actually behavior more typical of a four-year-old.

He was precocious in another way that irritated his parents: he kept asking to go into their bedroom. That usually doesn't start until after age three.

Part of the problem, which I got the parents to understand, was that because he was precocious and because they had high expectations of him, they looked at him as if he were a rational, reasonable person in the body of a two-year-old. They would try to reason with him. But he couldn't handle that, and the more he responded with his "stupids," the more angry and frustrated the parents became.

I tried to make clear to them that he had a need to protest and they had to recognize it, and also that they should not lose sight of the fact that, despite his protests, in the end he did what they wanted.

They learned to ignore "Get out, stupid" and not to grow angry over those outbursts. They heard him out and then told him, "Okay, okay, you do it anyway."

With the other problem, they were firm. "No, you may not come into our bedroom," they told him, period.

Much changed. To be sure, he still snapped his tough replies: "No, I don't want to. . . . You make me mad, stupid." However, he became quite manageable.

It all seems so obvious, but it wasn't to those parents, who didn't know that as a precocious child of twenty-eight months he was simply acting according to the book.

A very different case shows what might evolve if real chronic trauma occurs during this period.

The mother and son in this instance didn't come to me until he was over five, but the roots of their problem went back to when he was about eighteen months old, fighting with her over toilet training and being what I would consider normally resistant.

She looked at him differently. She was a rigid disciplinarian and took any signs of resistance as evil disobedience. "Ever since he walked," she told me, "he was a disobedient child." Her way of dealing with that was to hit him regularly. These days, we might call it child abuse.

Over the years she prevailed, and he finally got quite obedient, or so it seemed. Then, at about the age of five, he started to manifest his anger in quite an extreme way. He began to leave pieces of his feces in his mother's dresser drawers.

He was sending her a pretty clear message: "I'm going to crap all over you."

It took a few years of therapy for each to straighten things out. Like the other authoritarian mother I told you about, she had a problem with men, which was being transferred to the boy. Her husband was unloving, a troubled, heavy drinker. As she got a chance to ventilate her anger toward him and men in general, she loosened up on her son. She had less need to break him, was able to give him more autonomy. We also applied a couple of plans that got the boy out of the house more and more, away from that environment that was so punishing to him.

As I said, this was an extreme case, but in its excesses are elements that might be relevant to a more normal home.

BE FIRM, DON'T LECTURE

While I have been making the point that your flexibility in various ways is often necessary, don't misunderstand me. I certainly believe in reasoned discipline, in setting limits, and in being firm and clear with your child over what she is allowed to do and what is beyond the limits.

In the case above, the parents of the boy who talked back to them had a tendency to reason and explain with him.

Don't.

At this age your child cannot assimilate great explanations. If you want him to keep away from the light socket, you have to deliver that message with a simple, direct no. Don't try to explain to him that there is electricity coming through there, that electricity can shock, and so forth. Save the physics for high school. His attention span is so limited at two that he will simply disconnect your lengthy explanation from the dangerous act.

One mother came to me claiming that her two-year-old son was unmanageable; he was getting into everything and would never do what she wanted. The child had no sense of limits at home with his family, it seemed from her description, yet when I talked with the boy he responded appropriately to limits I set.

I was puzzled until I got the two of them in one room at the same time. Then I realized that this was a mother who could not say no.

"Now, darling, you mustn't play with that ashtray," she told the boy. (I was a smoker at the time.) "That belongs to Dr. Gabriel. And he needs that. If you play with that, you're going to get ashes all over you and Dr. Gabriel won't have anywhere to put his ashes."

Whatever she wanted the child to do was accompanied by a speech. The boy didn't know what she really wanted.

If I needed another clue, I got it when the mother told me that her housekeeper didn't have any such problems with the boy. He obeyed the housekeeper, she told me in a tone that indicated a source of her trouble. That was very distressing to her, as if the boy were rejecting her as his real mother.

But the problem was more with her. She was a working mother, possessed by the familiar guilt of being away from her son all day. One of the ways she compensated was that when she came home she couldn't easily give commands and tell him no, like a real mother. She felt that she owed him more. She had trouble denying him a pleasure, as if perhaps she weren't fully entitled to restrict him.

It wasn't easy for her to overcome those feelings. She came to understand them through counseling, but acting on her new insights was something else. In the end, it was their housekeeper, previously resented, who led her through her problem. The housekeeper showed her how she dealt with the boy—nicely, but firmly and directly—which reinforced what we had discussed in therapy in such a way that the woman was able finally to assume her proper role as mother.

PRIORITIES FOR BEHAVIOR

Let me summarize and expand on some points I've been making:

In this time of setting limits and laying down the tracks of discipline, don't bury your child in demands. There's only so much she can absorb. If you make everything off-limits and ordain that everything is to be accomplished at the same time, then nothing will be important to her. All will blur.

Establish a hierarchy of what's most important in terms of behaving and when certain things should take precedence. Have that clear in your own mind and make it clear to her by the tone of your voice and the expression on your face. If you scream and panic over the minor issues, you'll diminish the real importance of the big matters.

• At the top of the list, I'd put the dangerous stuff. Keep away from window ledges, fireplaces, stoves, electric outlets, stairways in houses, basement stairwells (I'm assuming you'll put drugs and poisons and cleaning fluids and the like out of her reach). Outside the house, never ever run into the street.

• Priority number two would be getting some reasonable toilet training: bowel control of some minimal degree, some daytime bladder control.

• Priority number three would probably be eating and messiness around eating. You can actually train a child not to be a total slob, but from fourteen to twenty months that shouldn't be a terribly high priority. It should wait until toilet training is pretty well completed.

• Depending on your own tolerance, priority number four might be less splashing and messiness in the bathroom. My own feeling is that children ought to be allowed to have a good time in the tub, splashing included.

TEMPER TANTRUMS, BREATH HOLDING

Breath holding is one of the most common reasons that parents come to me, yet I think it is rather underestimated as a serious problem in our culture.

I spoke earlier of the common garden variety of temper tantrum. Every parent should expect at least one, often a screaming, crying explosion, your child throwing himself on the floor, kicking his feet, banging his fists. It's scary.

The way to deal with it, as I've noted, is to ignore it. That's the greatest and most threatening form of punishment at this age. So literally turn away and, as you go, kind of over your shoulder tell him, "You're not going to get any cookie until you calm down and stop all that crying. And when you do, we can talk about what's bothering you."

You ignore the behavior until it goes away. If these tantrums persist, you can use the gold star technique, one star a day for each day there is no tantrum.

They usually disappear pretty quickly.

Breath holding episodes are something else. They are psychologically the same as tantrums, but they occur in children who are especially intense, usually boys who have very intense and somewhat aggressive temperaments. They are not nasty boys, just ones who anger easily and show quick tempers.

When they have a spell, they take a deep breath and hold it instead of crying. They hold it for a long time, turning red, then purple, then blue, and then they collapse. It is truly frightening, and often parents will take the child to the pediatrician to check for seizures. Actually, this is quite different from a seizure. There's no loss of urinary control, no rigidity in the muscles, no sleep afterward. It's almost like a mild fainting spell.

I don't have to tell you how terrifying it can be to have your child do this and pass out right in front of you.

For immediate treatment, as tough as it can be, try to ignore the child. If he actually does faint, pick him up and carry him to his bed, or wherever you were going when he started the breath holding. Usually, he'll wake up screaming.

If your child is subject to this behavior, check him out with your pediatrician and make sure—as much for your own sanity as anything—that these fits aren't going to seriously damage him. They won't.

At this age, they might continue for a few months, though I have seen them stretch out over a year's time, until a child is three and a half.

There are three approaches I suggest to such resistant behavior:

1. As soon as the fit is over and rational contact is possible, try to get him to talk about the things that anger him so, that trigger the fits. "Tell me what's the matter. . . . Don't hold your breath. That doesn't help anyone. Tell me why you're angry." Continuously repeat statements like that.

2. Use the gold star chart. It can be effective.

3. Try the "you're too old for this" routine. This sometimes works, though usually it's more effective with less serious behavioral problems.

BITING

Two-year-old David suddenly started biting his parents. They couldn't figure out why he had become so aggressive, and they couldn't stop him. Finally, when he bit another child, they came to see me.

What had set him off soon became clear. The parents

had taken a vacation for a week, leaving a grandparent to stay with David. She was his regular baby-sitter during the day, when they both went to work, but she wasn't accustomed to the longer hours this task required. By evening she was worn out, didn't have the energy to play with David as his parents did when they came home from work. So she put him to bed early without his high-quality fun. That was one thing he resented.

Much worse was that the parents went off without ever preparing David. They didn't talk to him about where they were going or, most important, reassure him that they would return.

Compounding this error, and David's anxiety and anger, they never called him while they were gone. They simply disappeared from his life one day.

When they returned a week later, he bit them. His response was an escalation of the more common response you can expect if you go away for a few days, even when you make an effort to reassure your child. She won't talk to you for a couple of hours or even days. Expect that and let it pass. A child, after all, has a right to be angry at being deprived of her parents.

Biting is not uncommon with two-year-olds, especially among aggressive, highly active, intense boys. It's their best weapon of offense.

It is also an extension of the orality we spoke of earlier. Babies, you will recall, use their mouths for practically everything. They put blocks, blankets, everything they can, into their mouths. It is a way to explore the world around them. It is also a form of regression to an earlier period, a way of coping with rejection and the anger related to it.

As they get older, some children also use their mouths to attack. Freud felt that one of the things that led to weaning was the child's inherent need to bite, a need that, when satisfied, hurt Mommy.

Biting and teething give a child pleasure, even if it is

a sort of painful pleasure. And the child learns very early that it can use its teeth and mouth as a weapon.

You sometimes see this come out with a child who is confronted with a new baby brother or sister. The sibling threatens the universe that was once all his, which makes him angry. In response, he attacks the cause and bites his sibling.

During the period we're now discussing, orality is being curtailed. Limits are being placed on it and on the pleasure it can bring him. He is told over and over he must not drink or put into his mouth anything in the medicine cabinet, anything under the sink, anything except food Mommy gives him.

This suppression continues, though children continue to have oral needs. Even when they are three, they might suck their thumbs. Indeed, most adults carry a certain amount of oral need with them later into life, which results in smokers, nail biters, even nose pickers to some extent.

Most children give up biting by the time they are thirty months old if they are rewarded for more verbal behaviors or if you admonish them enough.

Once again, the reward system can be effective, as it can be with any unwanted behavior. Give your child a gold star for every day he doesn't bite someone.

HONESTY

Don't lie to your child. It can undermine your whole relationship with her and turn her into a liar later in life.

Frequently, a parent thinks she is protecting her child from some of life's realities that are too unpleasant and unsettling for the little one. But that idea of insulating them is a mistaken one. Children can handle as much reality as you can give them. However, lies will shatter their trust in you, and will shatter your relationship. And children will actually learn to lie from you.

To me, lying is a conscious act that subverts the truth. It often starts with a small thing. "We're going to the doctor. Now, don't worry; he just wants to look you over. He's not going to do anything to you." And then he zaps her with a needle. It would have been far better to have told her, "I don't know what he's going to do. He's got to check you out, just like Mommy's doctor does to her." Then the two of you could have gone to face that particular life experience in his office together.

"This won't take a minute," you tell her, and thirty minutes later you're still at the neighbor's house.

"This isn't going to hurt," you say as you apply iodine to cleanse the scrape, and she howls.

"We're not going to leave you," you assure her; then you drop her at the baby-sitter's. That one is common and very damaging, reaching deeply into her fear of abandonment.

I do a considerable amount of work with children and the traumatic effect of major illness and surgery on them. I have had parents bring their children into the hospital for cancer surgery, for open-heart surgery, or for the removal of major organs, telling them all the while, "You're just going to a hotel for a visit."

At Tisch University Hospital in New York, we don't allow that kind of destructive deception. Imagine the crushing effect it has on a child, how much it can undermine her faith and confidence in those around her exactly when she needs them most, exactly when she needs a tremendous will to recover and live. Rather, we try to prepare the child psychologically for what's ahead by leading her into the truth.

I recall a few cases at another institution where children came from great distances—one from Europe—and their parents had lied to them. Because of the distances traveled, the decision was made to go ahead with the surgeries rather than send the children back home. The surgeries went okay, but the children suffered serious psychological problems as a result of the shattering deceptions.

Parents of a fractured marriage often employ a special lie: "Daddy will be home soon."

What is that child to think, to feel, when Daddy doesn't return at all?

We'll discuss the handling of a death in Chapter 5. So often in that situation, children are not told the truth. "Grandpa has gone away. . . . When will he come back? Oh, not for a long, long time."

Children at this age cannot comprehend the concept of death, but they can cope with the general idea that at some point our bodies stop working. And the trauma of loss at death is infinitely less for them than it is for adults.

I do not include as lies creations such as Santa Claus, Peter Rabbit, fairy tales, or widely held cultural myths.

To be sure, when those myths dissolve and your child discovers there is no Santa, it will not be a happy day for her. But she will get over it rather quickly.

But having told her about Santa, even taken her to sit on Santa's lap, will not have the same undermining effect, when the fantasy dissolves, as other deliberate and painful distortions.

Lying becomes a habit and it sets a pattern. If you want your child to be a reader, have plenty of books around your house and read to her a lot. Get into the habit of reading to her before she goes to bed at night. It becomes a shared ritual. If you want her to become a liar, start lying to her a lot. It will become habitual for you both.

With this, as with many other things we'll discuss, "do as I say, not as I do" doesn't work very well with children.

THE GREAT FOOD BATTLES: MESSY BABIES

When parents come to me because their babies make a mess with their food, I have a head start on the problem. The psychological problem, you see, is always with the parents.

A child between fourteen and twenty months is messy. That's normal. Of course, that normalcy can drive parents a little crazy, but I tell them, "Try to understand the nature of your child."

To start with, I should admit that I have little patience with parents who expect a great deal in the way of neatness from children this young, who try to impose adult standards of neatness on their infants. If they blame their child for not keeping his room clean, or for messing in his pants, I try very hard to disabuse them of their totally unrealistic expectations.

They might find it difficult to live with such "messiness," but as I said, that's their problem, not their child's. (Since I treat adults as well as children in my practice, sometimes the parent rather than the child becomes my patient and we figure out why that kind of "messiness" so disturbs her or him.)

At the same time, I'm not suggesting that you stand there and allow your child to pelt you with garbage. Nor am I suggesting that there's something wrong with you if you object to his throwing food all over the place. Nobody likes to have a child throw food around the kitchen, especially the person who has to clean it up. As natural as that activity might be for the child, it still is troublesome, and as you'll see, there are ways to cope so the throwing is controlled and eventually eliminated without breaking off the child's arms.

To start with, food to your child is not so much food as another thing for him to play with, a very pleasurable thing to play with. And play is a child's way of dealing with the world. It is how he explores the world and learns about it, by playing with it and its elements.

Food is a wonderful toy to him. It comes in all kinds of shapes, sizes, colors, textures—even hot and cold. He looks at it and says, "This stuff is terrific. I can mush it and I can mash it. I can shape it and I can toss it. And unlike other toys, if I feel like it, I can even eat it."

So there's all that special pleasure he's having—and, importantly, having at a time when he's continually trying to define himself in various ways, trying to establish a certain amount of autonomy. Again, from his point of view, he's doing something with his hands.

Meanwhile, I can hear you saying, the kitchen is a mess.

One thing you can do is give him dry food. He can eat it with his hands and still play with it, but the mess will be somewhat diminished. You can start with crackers, dry cereal, bread, cut-up fruit.

Also, quite simply, cover the floor around his high chair with newspapers. Suddenly, whatever blitz he unloads does not seem quite so much like the battle of Britain. When the meal is finished, you fold up the newspapers, toss them into the garbage, and your floor magically reappears.

Using a Spoon

Let him see how you do it, and when you give him his little model, he'll start to copy you.

Be sure those newspapers are all over the place. His motor skills are not yet ready to manipulate a spoon as well as you'd like.

Don't Push Too Much, Too Soon

I know you want to see him eating well, and if possible, doing it so your kitchen doesn't look like a slum after each meal. But don't push neatness too hard. Try to remember that this is also the time when you're trying to train him to use the toilet. In fact, if he isn't ready to use the toilet on a pretty regular basis, he's probably not ready to stop messing with his food.

Remember your own priorities. You've set toilet training high on the list for right now, perhaps at the top. There's only so much your child can accommodate. If he's trying to cope with this whole new thing of the potty, if he's trying to accommodate you by giving up that great instant gratification of going whenever he feels like it in his diaper to go in the potty, that's a major effort. If he's also now being expected, being ordered, to eat neatly, you might be overloading his circuits.

The Great Throw It/Fetch It Game

When you were training your dog, you threw a stick and frisky little Rex chased it down, brought it back to you, and laid it at your feet. As a reward, you picked it up and threw it again and he retrieved it again.

Now, in this feeding/training period, the same sort of thing will probably happen. Only this time your son will do the throwing and you will have the role of Rex.

He'll throw his cookie, have a wonderful laugh, and ask/tell you to bring it back.

If you like the role of Rex, by all means go retrieve that cookie. And you can expect that he will reward you just as you did the dog. He'll throw it again.

Unless you want to spend the day as the retriever, don't fall for the game.

Pick up the cookie, give it back and tell him not to throw it anymore. Depending on his development, you might tell him that you'll play that kind of game with a ball, outside, but cookies are not for throwing.

If he does it again, as he probably will, pick up the cookie and put it on the edge of the sink, on the counter, wherever—anywhere but back on his high chair tray.

He might howl, but after a while he'll get the message and stop throwing his cookie as if it were a ball and this were that throw/fetch game.

That's the good news.

The not-so-good news is that children at this age don't necessarily generalize. He might stop throwing his cookies but keep on heaving his cereal. Or he might, in fact, get the larger message and cut back on all throwing. At the least, you will break him of the cookie throwing.

Eventually, I promise you, he will abandon all such table manners. He will, given half a chance, actually begin to eat with a knife and fork in addition to a spoon. (I can't promise what will happen when he's in his teens or twenties, when he might start up all over again, this time with considerably more power, throwing his cookies, or more weaponlike items such as hard rolls, at the heads of his distant buddies across a crowded school lunchroom. That's another story, for another book perhaps, but I think such a vision gives fresh meaning to the word "regression.")

Pick Your Battlegrounds

Try to bear in mind what I said about priorities.

Before you pick up that cookie and throw it back at him in exasperation, remember that if you make everything into a confrontation, your life will be an unbearable endless war and neither one of you will be a winner. Oh, certainly, you will prevail. You are bigger. But you will not win.

I maintain that children at this age are just naturally messy. I'm not so sure, as Freudians maintain, that this messiness is rooted in toilet training and I don't know that it much matters. What we can all observe is that children are messy right through this period, that there are a number of ways we can control the mess in the name of peaceful coexistence, and that our expectations of them and the models we offer make them want to have better table manners by the time they are three (which, if you need hope and sustenance, you should realize is just around the corner).

It is also worth remembering that we're talking about a reflection of our particular culture. There are plenty of other cultures in the world where people young and old eat with their hands, all sharing from a large pot. I would guess that parents in those cultures set a very low priority on this whole problem.

THE GREAT FOOD BATTLES:
UNNECESSARY STRUGGLES

Conflicts between parents and children over what the children should eat and how much they should eat are bad for both and not necessary.

The first thing to remember is that your child will not starve herself. She has a very basic instinct to survive and she knows that the way to survival is through her mouth. She will eat when she is hungry. She may not eat as much as you like, and she might eat hardly any of the chicken or the broccoli, but she will eat.

If you really think she's not getting enough nourishment, and your pediatrician agrees, you can always supplement her meals with various chewable multivitamins, which these days come in appealing flavors and colors.

Unfortunately, I've seen countless situations where parents do not understand the basic rules of nutrition or the simple motivations behind their child's eating patterns. Instead, they become very controlling and turn each meal into a power struggle. "That child will eat what I tell her to because I know best and I know what she should eat and shouldn't eat," they tell themselves, invoking their finest dictatorial attitude. They are, however, ignoring the realities of nutrition and the nature of their child.

If they have, for example, a hard-to-manage child, they are likely to have a picky eater. One goes with the other, and there is nothing they can do to change it.

Furthermore, they are creating a major battle just at a time, as we've noted, when their child has a number of other demands being made on her, and, most important, is going through a search for autonomy. She is trying in her simple ways to identify herself and to get a grasp on her sexual identity.

All of this, just as we saw with toilet training, becomes wrapped up in the question of "How much will I give up to Mommy?" She knows she has to abandon some of her ways simply because Mommy is bigger, stronger, and tougher. She knows also that she'll lose Mommy's love if she doesn't adapt.

At the same time, eating is her primary, earliest pleasure. She is not likely to give up that pleasure and accommodate herself to someone else's tastes, even Mommy's, which are being forced on her, without a fight.

What can you do?

Urge her to eat, but be gentle about it: "Try some of this green vegetable. It's really yummy." And then let your case rest.

Let her experiment. Don't panic if she rejects one or another dish. Children switch their food loyalties all the time. One week she won't touch a piece of cheese, except perhaps to throw it on the floor. The next week all she will eat is cheese. "Try a little of the tuna," you say. "You love tuna," you remind her. Not a chance. She simply shakes her head and stuffs another piece of cheddar in her mouth.

Do not inflict any adult fad diets on her.

Above all, avoid a battle. Offer good healthy foods, coax, but rise above the tempting tug-of-war.

If you can do all that, you will win. She will eat enough to nourish herself on her own, while at the same time feeling that she has indeed protected her own identity. She has, if you will, decided something important on her own. In her mind, she has decided what she will eat. True, you have decided what goes on her plate, but she has taken it from there. So, in a way, you both win. That experience will leave her with a nice, positive feeling toward eating and toward you. The alternative, the screaming fight, will scar you both.

Some researchers maintain that the food power struggles of this period contribute to eating-related disturbances later in life, such as anorexia nervosa (forced, excessive, compulsive dieting and withdrawal from eating) and bulimia (compulsive, destructive, binge eating and self-induced vomiting).

There doesn't seem to me to be enough evidence yet to make an absolute connection, but certainly we know that anorexia does take place around the struggle for independence in adolescence. And I have treated a number of adolescent anorexic patients in whom the food struggles reach back to earliest childhood.

Enemas

A related, but today a much less frequent, problem is the giving of enemas.

Just as some parents insist that they know best when it comes to eating, some parents used to maintain that if their child didn't have, perhaps, two bowel movements every day he had to be given an enema.

That myth mauled a whole generation of children. There was absolutely no medical reason for the enemas, and children howled and fought and bitterly hated the things. Yet parents insisted and persisted, and won some kind of neurotic struggle; but everyone paid a price. Those high colonics destroyed human relationships and created horrendous problems later on. No child I ever heard of went mad because of enemas, but they certainly caused a great deal of heartache between parents and children and created a great deal of anger in children, which they had to deal with one way or another later on in their lives.

UNITED YOU STAND:
WORKING ONE PARENT AGAINST THE OTHER, OR THE NEED FOR A BEDROOM COLLABORATION

Toward the end of this period, when your child approaches thirty months, he's able to discern that what one of you denies him the other might give him.

It could be a cookie, a story, the permission to pull a game off a closet shelf, the right to mess with Play-Doh in the living room.

Little stuff doesn't matter so much, but for more important things, you and your husband should be consistent. If you don't want your child to eat certain foods, watch certain TV shows, get certain toys, the two of you should agree on those and stick to your decisions. I call that a "bedroom collaboration," because most often I find that parents plan their strategy behind the closed door of their inner sanctum.

Once again, your child is driven by his pleasure principle. He'll pursue whatever he's after and happily play one of you against the other to achieve his ends. Unfortunately, his effort can undermine your attempts at discipline, and it may contribute to the collapse of a shaky marriage.

I recall one case where parents came to me because, they said, their child was unmanageable. He was running the household and wouldn't listen to anyone. Interestingly, they didn't bring their little terror with them.

In twenty minutes it was pretty clear to me that the trouble lay with the two parents and their marriage, something I frequently encounter.

Although the woman said she wanted her husband to be more involved as a father, she claimed nevertheless that he was too strict and never let the child do anything. He basically maintained that discipline was part of raising a child and that all of that was her job, not his. His job, he said in a familiar lament, was working day and night to make enough money to support everyone. Meanwhile, in his view, she was not doing a proper job of disciplining the boy, nor was she doing the other work he expected of her, such as keeping their joint checkbook up to date, making phone calls for him, arranging their social life.

Obviously, he viewed the marriage as traditional. Although her own marital philosophy wasn't fully worked out, it was clear enough to me that they had basic differences over what their marriage ought to be. It was also clear that they had never discussed their views and reached a common understanding on their marriage.

The child was, quite unknowingly, able to play on the hostility of his parents toward each other to get whatever he wanted. If he went to his mother for something, she felt a strong urge to give it to him, to nurture him and overcompensate for her husband, who in her view was giving the child nothing of himself. Her feelings trapped her into overindulging the boy.

If he went to his father, the man would sometimes deny him and be intransigent simply out of anger for his wife. His inner response was, Why is this kid bothering me, why the hell isn't she taking care of this problem? When he was in such a mood, he would give a loud, mean no to whatever his child asked for. At other times the father would unconsciously subvert his wife by giving in to the child. "She won't let you have it? Of course you can have that."

The boy performed no such manipulations elsewhere. He did whatever his baby-sitter told him to do. He responded well to other children in his playgroup. His teacher and his pediatrician reported that he was extremely responsive to them, absolutely tractable.

When I learned that, I told the parents that he would respond the same way to them if they would only be consistent. But in order for them to reach that state, they had to work out the problems between themselves.

I recommended marriage counseling for them. Once they were getting along, it was possible for them to agree on an approach to discipline.

PETS

Parents often ask me if they should get a pet for their child, especially if they have only one child.

Pets are terrific, but only on one condition: that the parents want them and are willing to take care of them. Otherwise, forget it.

There is no way a child, even one up to the age of twelve, is going to be able to care for a pet in any responsible fashion. They have enough trouble learning to care for themselves.

Avoid getting the pet "because Alice really wants a puppy." If that's your rationale, and you haven't committed yourself to training, housebreaking, and taking care of that dog, you're going to end up angry at both your child and your dog.

I've seen so many instances where that happens and the parents become annoyed. They bought the dog for their child, they say, and the child won't take care of it, sometimes won't even play with it.

They made an assumption about their child they shouldn't have. Avoid that and the problem it brings by being sure, first, what you are willing to do in the name of a pet.

TELEVISION

I'll talk a lot about the effect of television on your child throughout this book, for obvious reasons. The subject of how much television is harmful to children is much debated. Generally, I am not of the school that says the box will turn your child's mind to mush, but I do have problems with excessive viewing.

Television is a dreadful baby-sitter. I know that many

mothers leave the set on all day as a kind of visual pacifier for their child. And it is that. But it is not a surrogate parent. It cannot take your place or that of your housekeeper. It does not for a moment take the place of healthy stimulation, play, or quality time.

It also gives your child the terrible idea that this is a good way to spend a day, numbed by a string of soaps, cartoons, and game shows. There is much more to life than that, as we adults know, and it is a parent's responsibility to be continually introducing a child to life's excitements and active pleasures, physical and intellectual.

A child at this age who is allowed to loll in front of a television set will develop the awful habit of doing just that. It will replace all other activities.

I believe in giving a child a balanced structure for his day. Television can certainly be a part of that structure, but there should also be time for play, for reading, for learning, for going places and doing other activities.

He should begin, even at the age of two, to understand that life is rich and varied, that there are all kinds of interesting and enjoyable things to do with your time, not just sit passively in front of a screen.

If you expose him to that kind of stimulation he will want to be engaged in the world. He won't want to spend six hours each day watching TV. Later in life, after you stop monitoring what shows he may watch and for how long—which I certainly believe you ought to do, as I'll discuss below—he'll be his own monitor. He'll watch a certain amount of TV, and be current with the shows all his friends are watching, but he'll also have many other things he'll want to do with his time.

Otherwise, he'll establish the habit of a TV sloth, and why not? That's what you've allowed him to become, grown accustomed to, allowed him to perceive as only natural and implicitly approved of. If, let's say, around the time he's six or seven he begins having difficulties learning, or problems with reading, and you suddenly wake up to the reasons why, you're in for a huge confrontation.

At that point, you're going to start screaming at him, "Turn off that damn TV. You can't spend the whole day watching TV. Practice your reading." Undoubtedly, you will have forgotten why and how he got into that rut in the first place. And he will be puzzled and angry that you are now turning on him and suddenly attacking him for no reason that he can determine. He is merely doing what he has been doing—apparently with your approval—all these years.

Television and Reading

There is little intellectual stimulation to be gained by your child from television—with a few major exceptions. These shows include "Sesame Street," "Mr. Rogers' Neighborhood," "Square One TV," "Pinwheel," and "Fraggle Rock." They are all marvelous for children, who love them because they are so entertaining. I love them because they stimulate and teach at the same time.

I have little use for the general run of cartoon shows that cram the TV channels on Saturday and Sunday mornings.

On one level, the quirky violence and bizarre fantasy worlds of those cartoons could be disturbing to a two-to-three-year-old. His grip on reality doesn't begin to take hold until the period between four and five. So, watching hours of cats exploding through windows, dogs crashing through roofs, and intergalactic humanoids zapping each other into celestial dust could leave him frightened and confused.

On another level, those hours are sure to infect him with the propaganda of commercials.

The cartoons, let us never forget, are merely excuses for the ads that totally surround them. And those ads are very cleverly crafted. Advertising agencies use all the market research and shameless psychology they can buy to figure out how to sell products to your naive, basically defenseless child.

The technique is fairly obvious. They try to entice and excite your child sufficiently about a candy that is bad for him, or a cereal that is bad for him, or a toy that is bad for him, so he'll go running to you, begging for the junk. If you say, "No, that's just junk," he'll give you an argument. After all, he's just been hooked, sold by a shrewd pitch. It couldn't be junk if it looked so great on the screen, he figures. It never occurs to him, of course, that the same wonderful TV set that shows him all those fascinating crashing cats would ever show him something that isn't good for him. Such is the fleeting innocence of children.

You can spare him the abuse of the advertisers and yourself the aggravation of arguments very simply: don't turn on those shows. Remember, at this age he probably cannot even turn on the TV set by himself. Even if he can reach the button, you should certainly have a strong rule that he may not watch anything unless you say so.

Indirectly, television will affect your child's attitude toward reading. How that happens is an extension of what I said above on the effects of overviewing.

Lots of parents of older children have complained to me that their sons and daughters don't read. Not too surprisingly, when I poke into their family patterns and histories, I find a whole lot of TV viewing and very little reading as the norm in their homes.

If you want your child to read, to take to it naturally and enjoy it, start reading to him early. At somewhere between twenty and thirty months, he'll be able to listen to stories and look at pictures and comprehend what's going on. So, if you start reading to him then, instead of allowing him to gape in front of a TV set, you have a good chance of channeling his interests to books.

Having books around the house will help. They will

be absorbed as a natural, friendly part of the environment.

Seeing you and your husband read is also important. You are the models, remember. If he doesn't see you two reading newspapers, magazines, books, a major link with the act of reading will be missing for him.

Models and encouragement and exposure to books, to writing, to learning, are critically important to his intellectual growth.

Many of the problems children have with reading and learning in general, I'm convinced, evolve because they are never motivated; they never become interested in reading or writing or learning. They don't get exposed to it in their homes; there's no interest or value placed on it in their families. Instead, everyone sits around and watches TV.

Reading to your child before he goes to bed can not only develop his desire to read and facilitate his connection with books, it can become one of your intimate rituals, something the two of you share and look forward to. And as he gets a bit older and begins to struggle with various fears and minor phobias about the dark, a short reading session just before he goes to bed will calm him and be therapeutic.

It will also be therapeutic for you. Reading to your child is one of the joys of parenting. There is a kind of quiet bonding that goes on between the two of you at those times, a special, private sharing. What a great calming cloud to sink into after a trying, tension-filled day. Savor it, even while you guide your child into one of life's greatest pleasures.

Television and Violence

As I'm sure you know, there is much controversy over the effect of TV violence on children. So far as I'm concerned, there is not sufficient evidence to prove that violence on TV is harmful to your child.

It can, however, affect her, especially around the ages

of three to four, when she's very impressionable and is beginning to understand what's she's viewing. It is also a time when she is given to a variety of violent fantasies and fears.

TV violence can feed into these fears. It can scare and confuse her. Do people really walk around on the streets shooting each other? Are those monsters real?

If she watches those dreadful soaps and sees the awful physical and psychological violence with which characters regularly abuse each other, that, too, can frighten her. It can also be a contributory influence on her view of life.

But overall, I am less concerned with the effect of violence on her than I am with the effect of TV slothfulness, of her becoming accustomed to hours and hours every day in front of the set, to the exclusion of life's truly vital and engaging activities.

How Much Television? You Decide

You can avoid the problems I mentioned above by simply taking charge of TV viewing in your house early on.

Start with your child's first viewing time, at around two years. Establish a clear pattern. You and your husband should decide which programs may be watched and for how much time. You two maintain the right to turn on appropriate TV shows and to limit the amount of viewing time. Perhaps there are even some hours when TV viewing is purely an adult function, and other times when it is for children.

I'd pick your child's shows until he is seven or eight. By that time he is through the age of reality testing, and he should have a good grasp of what is real and what is not. After that, I don't think television will profoundly affect his sense of what is real. But between the ages of two and seven it's better to be safe than sorry.

If you establish such a routine in your home, your

son will never develop the TV habit and grow accustomed to complete autonomy around a TV set. Instead, he'll have developed some good habits in relation to TV viewing, and you won't have to engage him in a massive power struggle at, say, age seven, when you want him to cut back on television and increase the time he spends on reading and learning.

CHANGING SURROGATES

Earlier in the book, I discussed the minimal effect on your child if you should decide to change your housekeeper. Up to the age of six to eight months, the connection between your child and your surrogate is not all that strong. Your baby might be able to distinguish the housekeeper's face as a friendly one, and indeed, the housekeeper might well have developed deep feelings of her own for your child. But the baby doesn't yet have the faculties to have forged the kind of meaningful relationship that, were it to be broken, would be painful and threatening to her.

Not that I recommend a regular changing of the guard during that period. After all, the basic idea of having a housekeeper is to create close relationships—among you, your husband, and her; between her and your baby. Obviously, that can be done only over time.

After eight to twelve months, your child will experience separation anxiety if your housekeeper suddenly leaves. By twelve to fourteen months, you may recall, she is experimenting with separation on her own. To the child, when the housekeeper disappears, it's a little like one of the child's own separation experiments with a terribly frightening ending. The woman who stands in for Mommy all day when Mommy is at work goes out of the room—and never comes back.

Making matters tougher for you is that at this stage your child can't talk, can't tell you what's disturbing her, and she can't yet comprehend your explanation of where the housekeeper has gone.

A two-year-old will perceive the housekeeper as another member of the family. If she leaves after a year or a year and a half, during which time the two have become deeply close, the child will become quite anxious and regress, falling back to an earlier period. You'll see her get increasingly babyish.

In the next period, when she is three, you'll see a mix of responses. You'll see anxiety; she's worried about who's going to take care of her. You'll also see remnants of stranger anxiety. What stranger will be coming in here? What will she be like to me?

If the surrogate was around for some time, you might also see traces of mourning, whining, crying, sadness, asking for the housekeeper. Your child really feels the loss of someone close to her.

At this age, you have a way of softening the anxiety and pain that you didn't have before. There is now language between you two. You can explain to her that the housekeeper loves her, but . . . Perhaps she had to take a new job closer to her own home. Or maybe she takes care of children under three only, so she had to go to a new baby. Keep it simple, but give her something that will let her begin to comprehend and cope with the problem.

The older your child gets, the more mourning and the less anxiety you'll find when the surrogate leaves. The child is able to understand more and has rational ways of dealing with loss as well as having new people in her life. She also possesses a greater sense of self and of independence.

Once your child is relatively independent, at around age seven, her relationship with a surrogate takes on a different quality. It will still be close and warm, but it is no longer such a matter of life and death for her. At that point the changing of the housekeeper will not result in as much anxiety.

In general, it is much better for your child—and for you and your husband—if you can keep a surrogate for a number of years.

Continual changes, as happen in some homes, contribute to an unstable environment. That disturbs your child's sense of balance. She is uncertain and insecure. Without being able to articulate it, she senses that just as she seems to be making a new attachment with a woman who has a major role in her life, that woman goes away.

If it happens once or twice during the first three years, your child will adjust to the change, with the responses I mentioned. But more than that, and I worry. Partly I worry because it usually indicates there is further instability in a household. Why can't the mother and father in that home make the right judgment with a housekeeper, I wonder? In Chapter 1, we considered the numerous steps you can take to give yourself the best chance of selecting the right one for your home. Obviously, anyone can make a mistake. But it is possible to find someone who can do the job and with whom you and your husband can feel comfortable.

Continual changes suggest any number of potential problems in the home that are not the fault of the housekeeper. Do the mother and father agree on what they want in their housekeeper? Are they realistic in their expectations? Do they agree on how they want to raise their child? Do they agree on anything? Is their marriage unsteady? Does the mother have guilt and anxiety because she is working and not at home, and is she projecting these problems onto the unwitting housekeeper?

As I said, long-term care is better for all, and with an effort, it is possible.

VACATIONS WITHOUT BABY: II

In Chapter 2, covering the child from birth to four-teen months, we considered the effects on you and your child if you and/or your husband had to be away on a business trip (tougher on you than on your child; always try to have either yourself or your husband at home). It was also suggested that, during that stage, if you two feel the need of a vacation you should keep it to a week-end.

With an older child, your leaving can be more diffi-cult for her. It's hard for a child of three and under to tolerate more than four days without her parents. Re-member, this is a time when she's very sensitive to sep-aration.

That's not to say you and your husband have to forgo vacations alone. As a great believer in quality time for parents as well as for children, I recommend them—but keep them to a week at most.

And don't simply vanish. This might sound like gra-tuitous advice, but remember the couple I told you about who did just that, as incredible as it seems, and re-turned to a little boy who was so deprived and angry with them that he bit them nearly every chance he got.

Try to prepare your child and your surrogate. Tell your little girl where you're going, maybe even show her pictures of the place, or a brochure. Explain that you'll telephone every day. Even though a child under three usually doesn't comprehend the telephone, she still can be somewhat calmed if every day at, say, breakfast time, your housekeeper hands her the phone and says, "It's Mommy and Daddy calling."

That call, by the way, will also ease the guilt and worry you might have and allow you to reassure your-self that, in fact, your child is surviving without you. Some parents are so anxious about leaving their child that it doesn't make any sense for them to do it. What good is a vacation if you can't relax, if you are constantly worrying about the bundle you left behind?

Separations like this are easier for everyone, of course, if you have a live-in housekeeper or a relative who can stay at your house while you're gone. Otherwise, be sure you discuss your nightly routine with your sitter. Keeping to an established routine will help to stabilize life in your absence. Ask her to have suppers and baths at the regular times, be sure she gives the child plenty of playtime, and if you've established the lovely ritual of the bedtime story, make sure that she follows that as well. You might recall that the parents who came home to the biter had the child's grandmother move into the house. Granny frequently had served as a daytime sitter, but never had done it overnight. The vanishing parents neglected to fill her in on the child's nightly routine, which consisted of lots of high-quality playtime with both parents. So poor Granny didn't know what the child expected, and besides, she was too tired at the end of the day to do much of anything anyway. She simply fed the boy and dumped him into bed, which added greatly to the boy's deprivation and anger.

I recommend mild bribery during your vacation. One couple I know invented the "secret messenger," who mysteriously brought a small, inexpensive toy or gift each night the parents were away. It was left outside the door of the apartment, and every morning the little girl woke and raced to the door to see what the messenger, sent directly from Mommy and Daddy, had brought her.

Before you go, tell your child that when you return you're going to bring a present, something special from the place where you'll be. And at all costs, don't forget to bring it back with you.

Even with all your precautions, chances are you'll get punished when you return. You might experience a day or two when your child simply won't talk to you. That's what you get for leaving her alone. But after and aside from that, 99 percent of the time, you and she will survive quite well.

4

The Age of Communication

(30 to 48 months)

I called the last chapter "The Age of Exploration" because, as we saw, between fourteen and thirty months, your child quite physically becomes an explorer. Being able to move on his own for the first time, he crashes into the world that has previously been beyond him. There's a different kind of discovery going on in this next period.

The Age of Communication, the period between thirty and forty-eight months, is a time of intellectual and emotional discovery and expansion.

It starts with speech. Your child is really beginning to speak at this point. In fact, at this stage he falls in love with language. He is now going beyond those private noises the two of you shared, beyond the simplest uses of language—"Want ball"—to complete sentences and the expression of complicated thoughts.

It is also a time when he's fascinated with the way things work. The two are related. As his motor coordination improves, and with it his speech, he is also absorbing more of the world around him in a new way. He is looking at everything more carefully and asking more questions. "What is that? Why? How come my arm goes up? . . . Muscles? Muscles? How come muscles lift it up?'' He wants to know the names of things and add those names to his flourishing vocabulary.

There is a great show-and-tell quality in all this. You have to tell your child all you know about a subject and he has to show you all he can do.

There's a great deal of magic in his world at this stage, which Selma Fraiberg describes in her wonderful book *The Magic Years*, when your child is teasing out what is real in his world and what is not, what is fantasy and what is not.

His world is filled with goblins and beasts and monsters, and in his narcissism, the notion that the world revolves around him, he feels that his thoughts can do damage, or magic, that they can actually make things happen.

Reality and the storage of information about what is real and what is not real will slowly and surely turn him into a person with a sense of ''reality testing.'' But at the start of this period, his whole world is magic.

Take television, which when you think about it is a pretty magical instrument for all of us. He sits watching people and animals dance on that screen, and at some point he'll ask you, without even looking away from the TV, ''Mommy, how does that work?''

If you told him that there were little people and little animals inside the TV set, he'd buy it.

By the end of this period, that won't wash. Save the discussion of physics and waves and electronic relays until he is a teenager. It might be enough to say, ''A machine makes it happen.'' Don't feel with this one, or with any of his innocently complicated questions, that you must appear omniscient. If you don't understand how a car works—or the human body, or the TV— share whatever information you do have and be honest about the rest: ''I simply don't know what makes that happen.''

Your child is now also beginning to get a sense that he can do things better on his own. He has a sense of autonomy, pride in what he does, and he wants to show he is grown up. He's been through the stage where adults told him what to do. Now, with better sensory motor development, he can see for himself what he's doing.

To Freud, this was the phallic period, starting at thirty to thirty-six months.

There are two qualities common to children at this time that he viewed as phallic. One is showing off, showing that they can do things. And the other is their curiosity about how things work.

In his view, that curiosity related to the early mental mechanism of understanding and control. The child could now control his bodily functions. Not only that, he took pleasure from turning his bodily functions on and off voluntarily. So Freud deduced that if a child could do it, he wanted to know how.

Taken a step further, he analogized the phallus as a tool, and the little boy wants to know how that tool works so he can control it. He can fire it or not fire it.

Also part of the confluence of developments at this time is his awareness of the world around him and his relationship to it.

He begins to realize that he is not the center of the world. There are other things out there, and he wants to understand them. This includes sexual things.

Having previously established a sexual or gender identity, he is now looking at subtle differences between the sexes. And he is looking with the refined sensory apparatus I mentioned.

To be sure, his interest is still simplistic and primitive. He wants to know, for example, why genital organs are different, not how you use them. He wants to know where babies come from, not how they are made.

At this age children of both sexes are intrigued by their own bodies, and boys especially with their external genitalia.

Boys and girls want to play with their genital organs, and they discover pleasure from doing so.

Many parents become alarmed and confused by this infantile masturbation. They aren't quite sure what to do about it, if anything. There is, or was, a school of thought that feared that if they tried to prevent it, they would repress their children and contribute to a sexual neurosis.

In fact, as we'll see later in the chapter, limits certainly can be placed on a child so that he can still be able to satisfy his natural curiosity yet understand that there are certain behaviors that are not done in public.

The notion that any sexual inhibition at this stage would damage the child was really a distortion of what psychoanalytic thinkers were once saying to a sexually repressed society. So-called progressive parents misinterpreted the intended message. They decided that their own uninhibited nakedness and total immodesty around the house, permitting their children to behave in ways that were not acceptable in society—playing with themselves in public, for example—would allow their children to grow up without any sexual hang-ups. But that was nonsense.

What the psychoanalysts were saying was quite different. At a time when elements of society perceived any sexuality as unpleasurable, a negative act, the psychoanalysts were saying, not so, it could be enjoyable. You could have fun with it, which is what children do with it. This is an altogether different position from having no inhibitions, no restrictions on your sexuality.

Culture and society now begin to intrude on your child as never before.

As I noted, his language is no longer private. It is the language held and understood by those around him.

Television is a carrier of culture and can obviously affect his language. You can take great advantage of his curiosity and desire to learn at this time by guiding him to the TV shows I mentioned in the last chapter and keeping him away from the junk.

Culture will have its most profound affect during this period for many who begin nursery school and who, for the first time, separate from parents and home.

Along with this comes a veneer of civilization you probably will want to apply. "No, you can't take your clothes off in the middle of nursery school." Or, "At snack time, don't just grab and eat. Wait for the teacher to give your snack to you."

Moving into the world at large brings a whole new condition for most children, playing with other children, and with it come some new rules. Up to now, most children, unless they have siblings, have been playing by themselves. They have no concept of sharing, certainly no concept of losing. They have no idea what it is to survive with other children. You may well find that you soon have to establish an important new rule: Don't hit other children. Show your instant disapproval of your child's bopping new friends: No hitting, kicking, or biting.

Conflict on this issue often is connected with postponement of the pleasure principle, which we discussed in the last chapter, but on a higher level. In this case, your child in nursery school might decide he wants the blocks. But someone else is playing with them. His response is "I want the blocks and I must have them instantly."

He can avoid pushing and hitting an innocent classmate to get them if he can understand that now he has to share blocks. (I assume in this situation that there is adequate adult supervision in the class and that bullies and extremely aggressive children are separated or controlled.)

The time from about three to five years marks Freud's famous Oedipal period. You will know that stage has arrived when you find your child standing by your bed in the middle of the night, or otherwise hanging around your bedroom. He wants to know what's going on in there because he has very strong notions of his own of what's happening, as fanciful as they might by.

There's quite a swirl of events within him at this point.

As we've seen, he's making great discoveries about his own body, including the fact that he can control his body.

Among all the new information he's gathered from his endless questions is the general idea that babies get made by parents and they stay in Mommy's tummy for a while.

With all his new sensory apparatus, he perceives that Mommy and Daddy have a special place all their own, their bedroom, and he's not allowed to go in there at night. He begins to imagine that Mommy and Daddy are having a lot of fun—skipping, jumping, playing games—back there in that room, and he wants to see and learn more about it. Feeding his thoughts are his limitless fantasies. For all his physical development, he still does not have a strong intellectual grip on reality. Factored into all this is the new event in his life, school. He is being separated from Mommy and Daddy.

In a sense, he builds his own theory about what's going on in your bedroom and why he's excluded. It's subtle. Children I talk to never speak directly of the mysteries of what Mommy and Daddy are up to in the night. They reveal their concern, perhaps, through play. They have two dolls playing in their dollhouse, and the mommy doll and daddy doll go into the dollhouse, but they lock baby doll outside.

That's a kind of spelling out of what is happening to them in their homes and with their schools. They are being separated from their parents, and they want to pull closer.

The issue of competition also comes into play. For the little boy, his prime objects in life have been his mother and often a female surrogate, and now it seems to him he's being forced away from his mother. There's only one person he can blame for that, his father. Father can become an ogre.

Some magical thinking gets sprinkled in here. They figure they can read your mind, and you theirs. Little do they know that when they begin to wish Daddy would go away or die so they could be with Mommy all the time, you really can't read their minds.

They begin to develop a lot of guilt around this desire to get rid of Daddy, and what we see in the Freudian interpretation is the development of the Oedipal conflict.

The little boy competes with the father for the attention of the mother. The boy develops guilt about that, which he has to resolve. He does, in a sense, by losing to the parents, by admitting that he can't have the mother and that he loses to the father. Unconsciously, he copes with the whole struggle by saying, in effect, if you can't beat them, join them. Doing so resolves an anxiety that grows in him out of his competition with his father, a castration anxiety. He fears that his father will mutilate or castrate him if this competition goes on. So he identifies with what he fears most, his father, and will become like his father in the hope that when he grows up he can get a girl just like the girl that married dear old Dad. It takes some two years for all of this to play itself out, and the boy gives up the fantasy of winning his mother.

It is through that experience that he develops a Superego, that he learns what society's rules are and develops a conscience, a sense of right and wrong. It is wrong to want his mommy.

Understanding how the dynamics of the Oedipal situation affected a girl was a problem for Freud, and it has remained a problem for many of his followers and theoreticians. Not only was his thinking incomplete, but his observations were strongly chauvinistic.

He saw the girl starting out with an attachment to her mother. But she couldn't just split away from her mother and become like her father, he felt. That would imbue her with masculine attributes, which didn't fit with his theories.

So what he evolved was the idea that she gave up her attachment to her mother because she had penis envy, a notion that has understandably brought upon Freud the wrath of countless women.

She wants to get her father's penis, one way or another, he postulated, by growing one or somehow getting one attached to herself. So she goes after her father and becomes very seductive, which, in fact, little girls of three and a half to four do. They become seductive and sexually playful with their fathers.

But now the theory seems to me to break down. Freud maintained that, out of their penis envy, little girls get very attached to their fathers, but they discover that no matter what they do he will not give them his penis. So they give up. They accept the fact that they are only going to be like their mothers. And reluctantly they become like their mothers for a number of years, until they gain their own set of special organs, their breasts, at which point they can truly identify with their mothers sexually. This lasts until adolescence, when they begin to break away and become independent of both parents.

As they do evolve through this experience, they become aware of the rights and wrongs of society and begin to develop a conscience, a Superego.

Fixed as they were on the idea of penis envy, neither Freud nor his adherents could allow that girls decide to become women for other reasons, because, for example, they decide that being a woman is just as good as being a man.

This is a scary period for your child, testing himself with new challenges, pursuing his curiosity. Out on the streets, he'll go off on his own, sort of, leaving you and running ahead for half a block.

Nightmares are common, usually connected with his explorations into your bedroom. His related fear of Father could trigger them, or his fear of separation.

Three widespread phobias of this age are the dark, dogs, and elevators. These stem from monster phobias and fears of loss of control. Expect them in your child, and remember: when they are mild, they are normal, minor, and passing disruptions, easily dealt with. A petting zoo might help ease him over his fear of dogs, and a nightlight can take care of his fear of the dark. If he squeezes your hand and grabs your leg each time you go on an elevator, no great damage done.

Despite this wave of anxieties, your child will still have a desire to do more, to master. So, he climbs to the top of an even bigger slide, and seeing what dizzying heights he has taken himself to, he breaks into tears.

This is the everyday stuff of the playground, and you have to do a bit of balancing with it. On the one hand, there is no question that you do not want your child putting himself into serious physical danger, yet he ought to be able to indulge his desire to push himself. And he ought to learn for himself that there are some things beyond his limits.

So, up to a point, let him get into trouble. He is discovering and establishing his own limits. Let him try a new, bigger swing, or go higher up on the monkey bars, or learn to ride his bike. You or your baby-sitter should be nearby, in case you should be needed.

To shield him and overly protect him will only lead to other problems and make his transition into society more difficult.

It is a transition, by the way, that some parents find very difficult to allow. They don't want to let go of their children. I find this especially so of mothers with only children, which is not so difficult to understand but is important to guard against, if you have such a tendency. It is your child who will pay in the end.

Let's look at how these principles come into play with specific everyday situations.

THE REAL WORLD

LISTENING TO MAGIC

It's important that you listen to what your child is saying and that you don't confuse her prelogical creations with lies.

Her vocabulary is growing, as we noted, but her thought processes do not keep up. That magical thinking, or what Piaget called prelogical thought, will cause her to answer your perfectly reasonable question— What's happened here?—with a completely fantastical reply.

She is not, however, lying. Often parents misunderstand and get angry from such an exchange.

Rather, try to listen closely and respect her communications, and translate them for yourself into logical terms.

I remember one day when I took a group of medical students into a nearby park to observe children at play. There were three mothers sitting on a bench, chatting, and one little girl came running over to them in great excitement. She had found a hairy caterpillar, and she began to describe it in the typical fantasy style of a three-and-a-half-year-old.

"I found a snake," she said, "and the snake has hairs, and the hairs are poisonous and it's going to grow up to be Puff the Magic Dragon," and on and on.

The first woman on the bench was not her mother and simply turned around and ignored her. The second woman, also not her mother, got visibly upset, became pale, rose and left.

The third woman was her mother, and she was terrific. She sat and listened to the whole story very carefully, and then she tried to help her daughter understand what she had actually discovered.

She gave it a name, a caterpillar, explaining that even though it might look like a tiny snake, it was really a caterpillar. And it wouldn't grow up to be a dragon, but a butterfly. . . . What's a butterfly? One of those pretty things we see flying around the park. I'll be sure to point one out to you. . . . No, the hairs aren't poisonous, you don't have to worry about that.

She was a wonderful example of a parent really listening, and she did what I urge all parents to do. The response of the mother who turned away is also worth noting.

If your child comes to you with a caterpillar or some other creeping thing, and you show revulsion, you'll teach revulsion. You'll convert her interest in some insect into a fear of it.

WATCH YOUR OWN IRRATIONAL FEARS

There is a difference between fear and anxiety.

Fear is a realistic avoidance—or fright-flight, the neurophysiological response to a real threat. Someone attacks you with a weapon. You are fearful and you flee, or you fight back.

Anxiety is the fear of an unreal threat—for example, that you are going to be attacked by an armed killer if you go out of the house.

You want to teach your children to have rational fears: Don't talk to strangers. . . . Don't ever run into the street. . . . Be careful of your private parts and don't let anyone touch them.

But there's a great difference between that and breeding anxiety in your children. Children at this age are easily frightened, and you can quite unconsciously turn anything into an unreal threat: Bugs are bad. . . . People who wear glasses are different. . . . People with black (or yellow or different-colored) skin are dangerous. The roots of prejudice are conveyed to children by parents who are themselves irrationally anxious about some race, some religious group.

Some children are brought to me because they have a school phobia. They are afraid of the place and don't want to go. But as I talk with them, I quickly see that their phobia is not limited to one thing. They have a whole bag full of terrors, which inevitably they have collected from their parents, who are in turn afraid of everything.

The mother of one of these children, I discover, spends twenty minutes each morning telling her daughter what to be afraid of when she leaves home. There are cars, of course, and strangers. And dirty dogs and other sources of germs. Be sure to take your lunch and don't trade any of your sandwich with any of the other children because you never know what you're going to pick up.

Over the months and years these caveats are woven into a remarkable tapestry. Certainly it includes animals. Mice are monsters; snakes are evil serpents.

Children apply their own fantasies to this litany of the horrible, and it can render them anxious about all of life. If practically everything is threatening, it's no wonder a child doesn't want to go to school.

At this age children are somewhat phobic to start with. We spoke of Oedipal competitions and conflicts. From that fear, they invent extravagant punishments for themselves. They go into their parents' bedroom, and if Daddy doesn't like it he'll kill them. Routinely they have frightening fantasies and nightmares.

If an anxious parent uncontrollably dumps her own phobias onto that monster imagination, the result will be a totally terrified child, afraid to do much of anything.

So, try to examine and watch your own anxieties. It's not always easy to do. Normally I find that when a phobic child comes into my office, it's not enough to treat the child alone. The parents have to be included.

DON'T IGNORE, DON'T RIDICULE

I spoke earlier about listening to your child and trying to enter his magical world with him. Your interest will feed his own natural curiosity of this stage, support him in his explorations.

But if you ignore him, you convey the message to him that he simply isn't worth very much. If he gets this message enough times, he's going to lose his initiative and interest in finding out about things, unless he's an unusually inquisitive, driven child.

Even worse is habitual ridicule, a behavior pattern I find with parents of disturbed children who come to me in their teens. The pattern has its roots way back when the children were three and four.

These are parents who frequently can't cope with their own feelings of competition with their children, so they put them down, ridicule them over and over. "That's ridiculous, utter nonsense. . . . You're such a foolish, silly child."

I've treated a number of cases of boys wrestling with homosexuality where this ridicule was an important component in a whole assortment of abuses heaped on them by their fathers.

I recall one case in which a father was trying to live through his son, wanted his son to be a great athlete. But the boy was not one, and never would be. The result was continual abuse and ridicule from the father: "You're no man, you're just a baby. Why do you do that? You should know better than to do that. You can't do anything right. All you ever do is make messes. Go on, cry and run to your mommy. Little mommy's boy, that's all you are anyway." Such an onslaught is one of the worst things a parent can do.

Perhaps even crueler is the silent treatment, total rejection.

It's not all that common, fortunately, but some of the most depressed patients I have ever treated suffered from this. They had parents who wouldn't talk to them for weeks when they were children.

One woman was a law student who couldn't handle any criticism. She was a brilliant student, but the slightest drop in a grade and she'd lock herself in her room for days. Her friends finally got her to come to me, and what I found, among other problems, was that her family didn't want her to be in law school—and whenever she had done something as a child that her mother didn't approve of, her mother had refused to talk to her for weeks.

In contrast to all this, you can help your children to stay curious and inquisitive, to explore and grow, and make them feel wonderful about it. And one of the best ways of doing it is to listen to them and be involved with them. They'll feel the difference and it will have a positive impact as they struggle through this difficult stretch.

THE SUBTLE COMPETITION

One of the subtle developments that evolve in this period is competition between you and your children.

It happens quite unconsciously.

For example, your child begins to assert herself and her interests. She wants to paint all the time. You want her to be more social, to play with other children more. You want her to be more active, to get into dancing. She goes to ballet class one afternoon a week, but it is clear from her and her teacher that she is not much interested.

You grow angry. Here you are, offering her the best of everything, and she wants to sit in a corner and draw rainbows.

It could well be that as a child you weren't terribly good at dancing, and although you don't even recall those days, there is something driving you to force your daughter to succeed at it.

I've had cases where a childhood of deprivation unconsciously motivated a parent. In a kind of classic situation, I recall one father who grew up in a slum, had to go to work when he was seven, managed to get himself an education and to become an extremely successful businessman.

He was pushing his son into everything he never had, especially athletics, and his son wasn't going for it. "I want him to have all the opportunities I never had," the father told me, "and that damn kid won't do what I tell him to do." Great hostility and a power struggle had developed between the man and the boy.

There is also the competition that springs out of the most natural and innocent sources.

This is a time, as I've noted, of enormous intellectual curiosity for your child. She is continually asking questions.

It can spill over. She can ask questions you can't answer, and unconsciously a feeling of rivalry arises. One mother told me that her daughter was continually making her look stupid in front of others, asking questions she couldn't answer.

Money can also fuel such friction. Remember, this is a period when costs can escalate. For the first time, she is going to nursery school. And for many parents that added financial burden causes them to apply new pressures on their children to shape them in certain ways. It's as if they are sweating to get more from their investment.

The struggle intensifies, unless you are attuned to it. It's easy to cross the line between disciplining your child and demeaning her. There's a great difference between yelling at her ("You don't appreciate anything we're doing for you, you brat'') and firmly scolding her for not standing on the sidewalk until the light changes.

It's so easy to let such anger overcome you. You see yourself and your husband making all kinds of sacrifices of your money and your time and all your energy, yet there she is, apparently oblivious to all that. She's going off on her own.

Yet, all is not lost just because her own talents and true interests are beginning to develop in ways that don't coincide with what you had in mind. You still can have a mighty effect on her. But you won't do it through a power struggle that is rooted in your own past and your unconscious feelings of competition.

EARLY CULTURAL CONFLICTS

Sometimes this subject comes under the heading of "manners."

You want your child to behave a certain way when you take him to visit a friend. You want him to dress accordingly. Perhaps you take him to a restaurant and want him to behave, not to mention eat with a fork.

I don't believe in overdoing this, but if you start at this age, expect resistance. Your child is being asked to do something that is often against his will.

That in itself will cause him to be angry. However, he might unload that anger simply by mouthing off. Try not to respond in kind. If he says he definitely doesn't want to wear any stupid jacket, stupid ugly jacket, that's okay, so long as he then proceeds to wear it.

We encountered this kind of situation earlier with the parents who had a little boy who kept calling them stupid and protesting nearly all their requests and commands, but who then predictably ended up doing what they wanted.

Those parents were still terribly upset by the fact that their son was so "disrespectful." They missed the point—and that is that children ought to have the right to protest verbally and not be punished for their protests and grumblings, so long as they end up doing what you want.

Of course, they won't always be willing to grouse and comply.

He doesn't want to go to the pediatrician, period. Don't bribe with that sort of thing. If all your pleading is ineffective, let him continue his grumbling and pick him up and carry him to the doctor's office.

Most three-year-olds want to show their parents that they can be good. They should be fairly accommodating unless they feel overburdened, or unless what you're asking of them is truly frightening. So, real resistance requires a close look on your part at what you're requesting.

Also, if you have a normally accommodating child and one day he suddenly balks at everything, check him closely for early signs of a cold. He might simply be coming down with something.

HOW EARLY FOR NURSERY SCHOOL?

There's quite a bit of pressure these days to place your child in a nursery school by the time she is three or a bit older.

Some children are ready for it at this age. Some who have not had much exposure to peer groups, have had only you or one housekeeper up to now, or are slow to warm up, might need more time before separating and plunging into that world of grown-up children.

If you try nursery school and find that your child after a week or two in the classroom still can't let you go for a couple of hours, think about giving up for a few months and then trying again. Just as you did with toilet training, don't force it.

Such resistance, by the way, has absolutely nothing to do with intelligence. I have known absolutely brilliant people who had trouble separating at the age of three.

MANIPULATION

A child can read his parents. Even before he can talk, he begins to read facial expressions and responses and he senses which parent is a pushover and which is a toughie. Quite naturally in pursuit of his pleasure, he uses that information.

Consistency between you and your husband is essential, or order and discipline can be unknowingly sabotaged.

If you say to your son it's bedtime at eight, both you and your husband have to know that it is eight and agree to it. If Dad comes home and your son asks him to play a game and Dad says, sure, let's have another game and then a story, Dad has been manipulated, you are undermined, and control is cracked.

If the rule is take all you want, but eat all you take, then you both have to stick by it when your son tries to get around it by asking Dad if he really has to eat his broccoli.

In our society, mothers are usually the pushovers, more bendable to pleading and cajoling. Don't get me wrong. I'm not arguing for rigidity. Flexibility is okay, so long as you both are flexible together.

Otherwise, your husband will be undermining you and doing great harm to your relationship with the children, encouraging them to become disobedient.

Watch out for the undermining situation. Dad comes home, finds the children running about and carrying on and you trying to settle them down. They plead with him and he says, "Oh, let them do as they please. They're only children."

Instead, try to maintain a unified front: support for the other comes first. If one of you invokes some rule or order the other doesn't like, support the other on the first occasion. Then in privacy work out how you want to deal with the matter in the future.

It's not always easy. One father cringed when his wife sent their son to a corner because he had suffered that same humiliation over and over when he was a child. In fact, he was so disturbed by that childhood memory that he railed at his wife, shattered her effort at discipline—as questionable as her technique certainly was—and scared and confused his son.

Frequently, I find fathers being made into villain enforcers by mothers. "Just wait till your father gets home," goes the familiar warning. I think that's a mistake. It casts the father as an enemy of his children.

Good discipline can be achieved if Father is by his actions consistently supportive of Mother, if they can work as a team and be perceived as one by the children. When that happens, discipline will follow. Efforts by your children to manipulate will not vanish. But they will diminish and be less disruptive of the structure you're trying to create in your home for them.

(Manipulation and consistency become paramount concerns in divorce, as we'll see in Chapter 7.)

MASTURBATION AND NUDITY

Parents are often astonished at first when I speak of masturbation in connection with their three-year-old. I should define the term. Masturbation, which is common at this age, is not the adolescent or adult activity of masturbation to orgasm. In the context of infantile sexuality, this is any genital play that provides pleasure.

It can take a number of forms. Little boys feel themselves through their pockets or rub up against something. Little girls slide down a banister or, later, ride a horse. Piggyback riding often provides genital pleasure. At this stage, boys are especially curious about and aware of their external genitalia and discover pleasure from playing with themselves.

That's natural, but our society tries to set some rational limits on it. It's not acceptable to walk around masturbating, or to do it in public. And there's nothing wrong with simply telling your child that. There was a time when any sort of sexual repression or guilt was thought to result in neurosis. But that's not believed today.

If you should come on your child masturbating in public, what is the parents' response? I would tell him that it's not very grown up to do that out here, that grown-ups don't do that and this is a grown-up room and if you want to be out here, then you can't do that. If you're going to do that, it should be done only in private. You should respect your child's privacy. If you do discover your child masturbating in his room, do not make an issue of it.

I would not scream at him, and certainly not hit him, as was routinely done in another age.

In talking to him about this, I'd use the proper names for his genitalia. Almost all families have a private language for genital organs, but by this age it's time to say penis and testicles, vagina and urethra. Don't be surprised if you have a bit of difficulty using the official names. Many parents who think of themselves as extremely liberated tell me they do.

Nudity around the house is a related matter during this period.

I'm not concerned with prudishness here, rather, once again, with society's rules on modesty. So, "Nakedness in the living room, or marching around the house without any clothes on, isn't accepted by adults. In the living room, wear your pants, or your pajamas." (To make this stick, the same rules should be observed by adults of the house.)

As I mentioned earlier, there was a certain amount of misinterpretation of psychoanalytic theory some years back to the effect that such a restriction on nudity would lead to sexual neurosis. But it was and is a mistaken notion.

NIGHTTIME RITUALS

"Don't forget to shoo the monsters," the little girl calls out as her parent leaves her bedroom.

That's part of the ritual in one friend's house. Whoever tucks their three-year-old into bed also reads her a story, gets her a glass of milk, has a "talk" (a review of the main events for the coming day), and does "monsters."

That means standing behind the room's closed door, loudly ordering all the monsters to get out, and counting to twenty, by which time all the monsters have fled into the night.

"They're gone, all gone," Mom or Dad then announces, after which their reassured daughter says "Night-night" and quickly drops off to sleep.

It's natural for children to get a little anxious at bedtime, and a familiar routine helps them through it.

Fear of the dark is part of it, and your child can develop this fear at this stage even if she didn't have it before. Parents are often puzzled by this. They come to me with children who are having terrible problems once the lights go out. "But my daughter has always slept in a dark room without any trouble," a parent typically tells me. "Now she needs a nightlight and has nightmares. Why is she so disturbed?"

There usually is no real disturbance. The child has grown and changed. Now she has a new way of contemplating the dark. Before, all she registered was whether the room was light or dark. But now, with her prelogical thought, she can speculate on all kinds of things happening out there, all kinds of things going bump in the night.

Children also love the nighttime ritual because it gives them a chance to have you all to themselves. This becomes an especially meaningful and precious time if there are other children in the family. As I suggest in the section on sibling rivalry in Chapter 7, space out their bedtimes so you can give each child special individual attention. And reading often helps.

There might well be a bit of Oedipal competition played out at bedtime too. A little girl wants to keep Dad for herself, keep Dad away from Mom for a while. Or a little boy might hang on to his mother.

NIGHTMARES

There are two kinds of nightmare phenomena, and when they occur they are scary for everyone, but they don't normally indicate any lasting problem.

1. A nightmare is a disturbing dream that will cause your child to wake up screaming, often recalling fragments of the dream.

2. The night terror is an upsetting dream that can cause him to thrash and scream without waking up. It is occurring at a level of sleep so deep that it doesn't allow him to wake. He won't remember any of it.

There isn't much you can do when either happens except to hold and comfort him. Even if he is still asleep, hugging and calming him with reassuring words will help settle him. And you as well. These are very upsetting moments.

They are, however, quite common from ages three to six, and nothing to worry about unless they occur night after night. Four or five nightmares over a three- or four-month period is normal.

If it does go beyond that, and your child's nightmares recur more frequently, he is very anxious about something. The fact that he is suffering these nightly disturbances doesn't, however, tell us what his anxiety might stem from. Pursue that with your pediatrician.

INVADING YOUR BEDROOM

She wants to be in there. At three years, she will begin to fantasize in her own prelogical terms about what the two of you are doing in there, and she will want to be a part of it.

Her fantasies are not adult sexual fantasies, but there certainly is a sexual component in her desire to go into your room in the middle of the night. This is her Oedipal stage, and she wants to come between you and Daddy.

Don't be surprised if you wake up at 3:00 A.M. and find her standing by your bed, sleeping at the foot of it or outside your door, or even getting in bed between the two of you. It's very common.

Normally, the best way of dealing with this is by setting rules quite directly: No coming into the big bedroom if the door is closed. This is our room and you have your own.

Be firm about this, or you will soon find that you and your husband really have no private place of your own, no privacy in your own home.

In many homes, the big TV set is in the parents' bedroom. Special arrangements can be made for viewing in there, and there certainly might be times when the whole family will watch a show together. Or there might be moments when your child isn't feeling well, is very disturbed about something and needs an extra snuggle and special attention. That's all fine, and it might even dissipate her need to creep into your room at night. The point is that you and your husband decide when those times will be and still control the gate and key.

If you have had a situation where your child was sharing the space in your bedroom, by now you should really have made some other arrangements.

To a child of this age, sexual intercourse resembles an assault. She imagines that Daddy is killing Mommy because of her. How damaging this is to her is debatable, but to my mind it can't be healthy.

So, move her out and/or keep her out, and maintain the off-limits specialness of your own bedroom.

Nevertheless, morning cuddles—or cuddles anytime a child doesn't feel well—are perfectly okay, and Sunday morning bedroom visits are happy rituals in many homes.

GAMES

Children at this age simply have to win. They are in the phallic period or early Oedipal stage, remember, when they are both showing off and competing with you.

Puzzles work well, allows children to show how clever they are. So does any game with a large element of chance as opposed to skill. They don't have much in the way of skill, and because of their short attention spans they can't absorb complicated sets of rules. But in a game like Candyland, or any game in which moves are made according to dice and dials, the whole idea is luck. He has a fifty-fifty chance of winning.

Don't be surprised even then to see him improve his chances by changing the rules and cheating a little. Losing is a painful concept to him, because then he can't demonstrate that he is as good as his mother and father at something, that he can compete with them.

There's no harm in introducing the idea that you can have fun playing a game even if you don't win. But it won't really take at this age.

Avoid games of skill such as checkers. Playing any game like that with a four- to five-year-old is a form of hostility and ridicule.

I've had parents bring their children in and tell me what liars and cheats their children are when we talk about the games they play. But it turns out that these are parents who don't understand their children very well and don't know it. One of the ways in which they hurt their children is by playing checkers and other games of skill with them, and clobbering them game after game.

The children respond in part by trying to change the rules to give themselves a tiny chance of victory and retain a shred of self-respect. Often, they further respond by taking their fury out on all their classmates. As their parents clobber them competitively, they now clobber the other children with blocks and sticks, which is why they end up in my office—not always because their parents are concerned about that behavior, but because the school tells them that unless they get some help for their children the school will throw them out.

So, play plenty of games of chance and let them win as much as possible for a while.

DRESSING THEMSELVES

Selecting the clothes she'll wear that day and putting them on by herself are additional ways your daughter can show off.

That's all fine, but if you don't structure the process you can find yourself in an extremely drawn-out session of pleading and negotiating just at that time in the morning when you have neither the time nor the patience.

Bear in mind that at this age your child is only beginning to discern one color from another and has absolutely no idea of whether blue shoes go with brown dresses. Confronted with an entire closet full of dresses, she will quite likely cope with her confusion by selecting one, then another, then another and another, quite content to play out an endless ritual with you.

You can avoid all that if you limit her choice. The night before, lay out, say, two possibilities for the next day. If she wants more, negotiate. "First, show me that you can choose from two outfits. If you can do that for a week, then I'll let you choose from three."

This is hardly a major area of developmental conflict, but I have encountered a certain number of intellectual mothers who get ensnarled in endless 8:00 A.M. conversations over this. They mistakenly think they are abusing their children if they say, "No, you may not try on every dress hanging in the closet."

As I said, you can spare yourself that and also add to your child's sense of organization and structure, which is important. Children need and want a structured life, contrary to what those ensnarled mothers thought. Structure is not repression or punishment.

CREATING SUPERCHILD

This will boomerang. If you decide that you now want to teach your child the alphabet, basic reading, and numbers, all your efforts and good intentions can result in killing his initiatives and motivations.

Quite simply, he doesn't yet have the tools. He doesn't have the ability yet to connect numbers or read, or to sit still and concentrate for more than about four minutes.

If you sit him down and proceed with your lesson, he may sit there out of a need to please you. But he is numb, not learning anything.

Imposing that kind of routine can smother his initiative and develop in him a chronic loss of interest, chronic boredom. Boredom is a masked form of depression.

It's very different if you try to follow his lead and have a number of different stimuli available to him. Those work-bench-drawing stools are wonderful, with letters and numbers all around the margins of the blackboard. He can sit and draw on one side, play on the blackboard on the other, copy a few letters or numbers.

Or let him have plenty of crayons and paints, so he can draw when he feels like it.

If he shows a particular interest in learning the alphabet, that's different. Perhaps he has an older brother or sister who's doing it, and that stimulates him. In that case, by all means help him. There, and in any situation like that, follow his lead. But even then, try to bear in mind that his learning skills are limited. Don't overdo it.

CARS AND TRIPS

At three, your child is still not ready for a long car trip. Not that a four-hour trip is going to cause neurosis, but it is going to be very hard on you. An uncomfortable child is going to get restless, then yell and cry a lot.

If you have a choice, take a plane.

If you don't have a choice, break the trip up with several pit stops, chances for everyone to go to the bathroom, walk around, get a food treat. And bring plenty of games, tapes, and coloring books in the car.

I'm against Dramamine or some other anti-motion sickness medication for a child. A big dose of the stuff will put a child to sleep. However, if there is some unavoidable emergency when you absolutely must make the trip and you have no alternative but to take an active three-year-old, call your pediatrician.

5

The Age of Separation

(48 to 60 months)

It's called school and it represents a giant step for your child away from you and into society.

This is different from the nursery school we discussed in the last chapter, where we encountered the beginnings of separation. That was a baby step, a few hours of more or less structured play in the morning. Now comes the real thing.

Now comes prekindergarten and a full day of school, a full day of separation.

The extended separation and the many new demands society will place on your child will test him, cause him to wrestle with a number of adjustments. But it is not only children who may find this a bumpy time. For many parents, especially those who have not had their children in a nursery school program, this extended separation is a cause for anxiety and depression. This is especially true for overly involved and protective parents. They have a terrible time, and unfortunately their fear of the school and the threat it represents to them gets conveyed to their children.

In the school, society has new expectations. It expects your child to handle the full day's experience. It assumes that he can sit and do a task for a particular period, that he can get along with his peers.

The pressure to push children is great in our society, and it can cause parents to put their children into a full-day prekindergarten class before they are ready for it.

Resist that. Another year in nursery school might be just what he needs. It could let him grow that much more. It could let him avoid starting real school before he is really ready for it, when he could end up feeling lost and uncomfortable in it, overwhelmed by it. And you could end up facing the terrible decision of whether or not to have him repeat a grade.

There's a lot you can do to determine whether or not your child is ready for the more demanding class by assessing him in three general areas. You can measure his biological readiness, you can consider his psychological qualities, and you can weigh the cultural demands that will be made on him.

Let's examine each of these.

BIOLOGICAL READINESS

Activity Level In a full-day class, your child will have to sit down at times and perform a task for ten or fifteen minutes. It might be painting or banging on something.

Think about it. During the last year, has he reached an activity level where he can sit and do one task for fifteen minutes? By the time he's four, he ought to be able to do that.

Can he sit for fifteen minutes and listen to a story? That's another expectation his new school will have of him. Can he handle it?

This is different from nursery school, where there's a lot more running around and less demand for sitting and focusing on one project for stretches of time.

Toilet Training Has he mastered it yet? Again, by age four, that should be over, and many schools won't take him in a full-day class if it isn't.

Temperament In Chapter 2 we discussed temperament in terms of rhythmicity, activity, intensity, passivity.

His biorhythms come into play here because he might have an odd sleeping pattern and normally sleep till eleven in the morning. You might have to change this pattern so he can get off to school when it starts in the morning.

Or he might have trouble tolerating regular mealtimes. With a full-day class, eating at lunchtime becomes important, and you might have to adjust that.

At this age, he can and will adjust such sleeping and eating rhythms. You have to set the new schedules for him.

Physical Maturity Premature babies and others who are born small need extra years to mature both emotionally and physically. At the age of four, say, yours might possess perfectly normal intelligence, yet be smaller, frailer, less coordinated than other children the same age. That usually will not prevent a child from going into prekindergarten, but at the end of the year a decision might have to be made about sending him along to kindergarten or allowing him to repeat a year of prekindergarten.

I frequently consult with pediatricians about this situation, and we make our decision not on the basis that a child is failing but rather with a view toward letting him have the best possible chance to succeed in our highly competitive society. Life becomes especially hard for him if he can't compete on a physical level, if he simply isn't sufficiently coordinated.

Understandably, some parents find it difficult to keep their child back. I try to point out to them that if they don't, there's a good chance that their child will be the "D" child in class, a lousy experience for him to suffer, and one that can be avoided if he's given a little extra time to mature.

Hand-eye Coordination He needs a minimal amount

of this. He will be using a paintbrush, crayons, pencils. He will be expected to eat with a spoon.

Laterality By the age of four, he should have decided whether he is right-handed or left-handed.

Two-year-olds are quite ambidextrous; three-year-olds start to favor one side. It does not make any difference whether he settles on being right-handed or left-handed, and you should not try to force him one way or the other. But the matter should be settled by the time he's four.

Where a mother is left-handed and the father is right-handed, or vice versa, development is sometimes slowed. And there is a certain amount of mixed dominance in left-handed families. That results in some malcoordination.

Later on, some researchers are now saying, this can create reading problems. They maintain that because of this and a number of other developmental conditions up to 20 percent of children entering first grade are not prepared to handle the material. Of them, 75 percent reportedly work out their problems during the first grade, but that still leaves 25 percent—or a total of 5 percent of the child population—with significant learning difficulties.

Language Readiness Does your child speak a language only you can understand? Is he still communicating with infantile speech?

This will show up very quickly in prekindergarten, where other children are communicating easily, and where your child will be exposed to an objective adult assessor, the teacher.

I've seen numerous cases where parents haven't been aware of a language problem and a teacher picks up on it within a few days of class.

These are perfectly bright children who haven't got the motor skills yet for appropriate speech. Their infantile speech, which their parents have adapted to, is almost incomprehensible. They could need speech therapy.

PSYCHOLOGICAL READINESS

Weighing your child's psychological readiness gives us a good chance to look back and see how another developmental line works, this one originally described by Margaret Mahler.

Originally, you'll recall, we spoke about two phases, the autistic and the symbiotic.

The autistic lasted two to three months, a time when there was nothing psychologically for your baby but "me, me, me."

The next two to three months were the symbiotic phase, during which, in a primitive way, she began to respond to other people. There was more to the world than just "me."

At about six months, individuation began with what we call differentiation. From her crib she started to distinguish between familiar and unfamiliar faces, and we saw stranger anxiety: your mother came into the room and your baby cried. That went on from six months to around ten months.

Next came practicing, from ten to sixteen months. She began to crawl and explore to see what made up her own person and what was other people.

That led to rapprochement, from ages two to three. Now instead of simply crawling, she was actually leaving your presence, going into the other room, then coming back to be sure you were still there.

The extension of that was object constancy, sustaining an image or fantasy of the missing person. She could go away for hours, retain a mental image of you, and know that she had a mother to go back to.

It was that quality that enabled her to separate from you and get through a morning of nursery school.

Now she will have to be able to stay away from you

for five or six hours. Can she do it? If not, you can try the separation drill you began with nursery school. You or your housekeeper takes her to school and stays there, and little by little, leaves her earlier and earlier. It might take three to six weeks before she develops the object constancy she needs, retains a mental image, and is not frightened by the separation.

Another developmental line you should review is the one that leads to coping mechanisms, or what used to be called defense mechanisms, which were studied by Anna Freud.

We have seen these evolve throughout the book. In the beginning, your very young baby had only one coping mechanism: denial.

If she was hungry and there was no food for her, she denied her hunger and went to sleep.

As she approaches school age, her coping mechanisms will allow her to deal with situations without collapsing, withdrawing, or regressing. So, in the classroom if she's playing with another child and the child has a block she wants, but the teacher says it belongs to the other child, your child has some options. She can put the block idea aside and go play in the sandbox, which would be a displacement activity. Or she can fall into the corner in a fetal position and start sucking her thumb, which would be regression and withdrawal.

Coping mechanisms, in other words, are important in that they help her withstand the little stresses of everyday life and allow her to avoid acting on every negative impulse. The fantasy might have been to grab the block and bash the little boy in the head with it. Now she still might hold the fantasy, but she has more civilized ways to cope.

We all must have them. They are the veneer of civilization and let us all get through the day. How many times a day are you insulted, yet cope? Adult mechanisms are more varied and sophisticated, though their roots started to show in our early years.

Displacement, for example, occurs when you are angry with your boss for mistreating you, have a fantasy of yelling at him, and instead yell at your child when you come home. Displacement begins with three-year-olds, when they have the same type of fantasy toward you and discharge it by beating up their teddy bear.

In our discussion of divorce in Chapter 7, I note that children may be angry at both parents but tend to displace most of their anger on the custodial parent, who is usually the mother. She's there with them, and they know she's there. It's too frightening to them to act out against Daddy because he might go away altogether.

When your child is around five, you should begin to see what we call reaction formation, and indeed, if you find this, you have a very positive sign that your child is ready for school.

This is the quality you see when children begin to identify with one parent or the other—saying, in effect, "I'm a big girl now."

She is not really a big girl, but by unconsciously pretending to be she can dispel much of the fear of going to the big school. Reaction formation is sort of the opposite of what she is. She's afraid, so she's going to be brave, acting unconsciously or even consciously in a way that is opposite to her inner feelings.

Later on, it makes for Medal of Honor winners and race car drivers. For now, if she is beginning to act like she wants to be grown up, modeling herself after her parents, who, for example, go off to work, then she's also ready to go off to work, which is what school represents for her.

CULTURAL SKILLS

Some of these, such as toilet training and language facility, we've already touched on.

He'll also be expected to have some minimal skills in eating. A real school won't tolerate too much eating with his hands. And he'll need to have developed a broad enough taste in food to accommodate the school lunch.

The culture he's entering will expect a certain level and kind of behavior.

• He should be at a point where he respects the property of other children, where he is able to play with them. He will be expected to share with others.

• When he's told by a teacher, ''No, you may not play with that toy,'' he will be expected to listen and understand.

• Similarly, when he's told to leave another person alone, he will be expected to listen and understand.

• He will have to conform to a schedule, which can mean, as I noted before, being able to sit through a reading session or lie quietly through naptime. The hyperactive child will have a tough time fitting into such a regimen.

Let's examine ways to deal with some of the problems of this period.

THE REAL WORLD

EASING THE TRANSITION

If your child hasn't been to nursery school, think about day camp in the summer before kindergarten. Use the gradual separation technique. At first, you wait outside for the whole session, day by day, then begin leaving earlier and earlier.

A class at the local Y can serve the same purpose. It might be for only an hour, but it will get both of you accustomed to separation.

If your child begins to declare that school is not for

her and she has no intention of going, you can counter with a subtle propaganda campaign.

Modeling is useful. If you know of a slightly older child who enjoys school, engage her in a conversation about it at the playground, a conversation your own child can hear and participate in. Then remind her of it: Joanie is so lucky to be able to go to school, and soon you'll be old enough to go too. When you pass children on the way to school, comment on how lucky they are.

At night, after reading to her, you might tell her that when she goes to school she'll have a whole library of books to choose from.

The whole experience, in other words, should become something special and exciting that older children get to do.

It's also a good idea to take her along when you go to look at schools, once you have them narrowed down to two or three. There's more of a selection process, of course, if you're going to send her to a private school. With public schools you can generally arrange for a visit some months before starting.

Teachers at this level are normally very good at coping with separation problems, so if you sense this is going to be tough, discuss it with them beforehand.

And be prepared to be persistent. Your child might be angry with you for it, but it's highly unlikely the experience will lead to any permanent problem.

TESTING

Private schools frequently require that applicants be tested and interviewed. Unquestionably, the process is much more taxing on the parents than the children.

Most children have little trouble with any of it. Slow-to-warm-up children or others who are temperamental find it stressful, but others pretty much take it in stride.

The fact is that testing and interviews are part of our

society, and as children face society they're going to have to face such social stresses.

For parents, I find, there's real anxiety in confronting their child's capacities or incapacities. Furthermore, competitive parents invest too much of themselves in the success or failure of their children at this stage, as early in life as it is. As usual, if you are anxious, your child will pick up on it and a scary fantasy could well evolve—for example, one in which she will be scolded for not doing well enough on the tests, or for saying something silly at the interview.

Many parents play games and lie to their children about this whole process. It's going to be like a party, they say, and the whole thing doesn't matter much anyway. In a moment, the child can see that it isn't any party and can also sense that it does matter.

Don't lie and don't bribe them. Tell them that just as you and she are looking at different schools, these schools want to see what she's like, how she plays, what things she can do. The teachers will probably ask lots of questions.

She can handle that. It's not going to scare her. And she won't even view the whole experience as highly competitive. For her, it's a chance to try out a few things with a few other children in the classroom.

LISTENING TO YOUR CHILD

In Chapter 4, I spoke of the importance of listening to your child and sifting through his magical thinking and interpretations of reality.

With his new voyage into society, his reports are all the more significant. He is bringing back news from outer space, real news and fantasies, and his reports can enable you to pick up on potential problems early.

Again, you should be able to discriminate between his magical thinking and fantasies and what's really going on. Maybe he is having trouble sharing and playing in his new environment. Maybe he is having trouble learning.

Taken to something of an extreme, I think some of the recent disturbing cases of child abuse were hinted at by the children. Peculiar things were happening to them, they told their parents, or so I read in some of the reports. But their parents were either not listening or simply did not believe them.

Listening to teachers is important too. I find parents disbelieving and dismissive of reports from teachers when the material is not to their liking. The result can end up in my office some time later, a real learning or adjustment problem that might have been nipped early if the parents had respected a teacher's insight.

LEFT-HANDED/RIGHT-HANDED

As I've noted, there is no better, superior side, and you should not try to push a child one way or the other.

In life, it will not matter one bit which hand she chooses. There are wrenches for left-handed people and violins for left-handed people, refrigerators designed for them—and, for some strange reason, a vast number of doctors are left-handed, if that's what you have in mind for her.

What matters is that your child settles on one or the other by the time she is in the first grade, which means that you now have two years for that to happen, and you should watch for signs of which hand she favors.

The timing of the choice is important because once it's done she can begin storing information in her brain for tasks, such as writing, that require the choice. This is not to suggest that she is not learning anything until she makes the left-hand/right-hand choice. She is. But the evidence is that until she makes the choice, her ability to absorb the kinds of skills that schools teach, such as writing, will be limited. The ambidextrous child normally has greater difficulty and takes longer to store this kind of information.

School learning will come about as a result of information being stored in the dominant side of the brain, the opposite side from the hand she uses. So, if she settles on being right-handed, she will store information in the left brain, but that information won't be stored there until she decides to be right-handed. The non-dominant hemisphere is probably for her emotional life, artistic sensibilities, and a number of other things we're not so sure about.

While you can't or shouldn't rush her, you can keep an eye out for which side she favors and encourage her to use and settle on that side.

If she hasn't made a choice by the first grade, she might well have to repeat kindergarten.

THE HYPERACTIVE CHILD

Families often adapt so remarkably to a hyperactive child that they don't even know there is anything unusual about him.

He goes into full-day school, and by the end of day one the teacher is beside herself, screaming to the parents. Some of the most severely hyperactive children I've ever seen have come from such families, who turned to me after the discovery was made in school. These poor children can't sit still for five seconds. When they come to my office, in no time my papers are strewn all over the place, not because the children are angry or trying to be disruptive. They simply can't control themselves. It's as if their engines are uncontrollably overheated.

They can be helped, first by easing up on school. If they go back to nursery school, they are able to run around more and have fewer demands made on them. They don't have to sit through stories or be still for naps.

Then I work with the parents to structure the child. Maybe he can't sit for fifteen minutes, but he can sit for a short three-minute segment of "Sesame Street." So we start with that, and try to extend his control gradually.

There is also medication available, but I'm very conservative when it comes to such medication, and would certainly prefer the extra year in nursery school with a complementary program of time structuring.

Some of these children have serious learning problems as a result of their hyperactivity—an attention deficit disorder, as it's called. They can't concentrate. They require special tutoring in small groups.

Depending on the severity of their condition, many hyperactive children can make their way through school without special help. They're bright enough to compensate for their difficulty. They might be known as the class pest and disrupt things now and then, occasionally drawing official complaints, but by the end of the first grade they have made it. To be sure, they pay some sort of price in self-esteem for being the class nuisance, but intellectually they have broken through.

Others manage to stay in the class and learn, but with difficulty. They tend to hold up the bottom of the class, and occasionally show up in my office.

I WANT TO BE A POLICEMAN. . . . I WANT TO BE WONDER WOMAN

A friend told me about his four-year-old daughter. Her great passion was zooming around the apartment in her Wonder Woman costume, shouting "What's your problem, sir?" She would listen to his problem—preferably something like a cat being stuck up in a tree—wave her arms, and promise to solve it in no time, a nice example of omnipotent fantasy. Little boys her age are declaring that they want to be policemen or firemen.

All of this is related to an aspect of Oedipal development we considered earlier. About this time, boys are deciding unconsciously that they are not going to successfully replace Daddy. The coping mechanism and the underlying unconscious fantasy for this is to identify with the rival: If I can't beat him, says the little boy, I'll join him.

Issues of guilt, of good and bad, begin to surface. His conscience is expanding. He knows he can't romp into the parental bedroom.

The idea is to be good, and a policeman is that. He knows what's good. He takes care of good people. He gets the bad guys.

Later, the identification will be more direct, and if Daddy is a lawyer, that's what he wants to be too.

Girls follow the same progression, but the pattern is more subtle. Even by the time she's three, she can sense society's expectations and decide that she doesn't want to be a cop or a fireman. Some girls choose to be a good mommy and have lots of babies. Later, they identify more directly with Mom, and if Mom is a lawyer, that's also what the child says she wants to be.

SEXUAL CURIOSITY AND ABUSE

Who can't remember playing doctor as a child? That's an extremely widespread way for children at this age to indulge their considerable sexual curiosity. They want to look at themselves and at their friends of both sexes. And they want to look at their parents.

At this age, children also like to play with themselves, and as we discussed earlier, you can teach your child that private parts are not to be played with in public.

You can also teach them that they are the only ones who should touch their private parts. Children are generally willing to let a trusted adult touch them, but without terrifying them you can get across the idea that their private parts should be respected and simply not touched by others, their playmates, or even any friendly adults. Basically, it's a good idea to make it clear to your children that they should report it to you anytime someone tries to touch their private parts.

You don't need a lengthy, detailed discussion about this either. He might well ask if mommies and daddies touch each other. There's no reason not to say yes, but add the point that that's for mommies and daddies, grown-ups who are married, not for little children.

There is great concern these days about the sexual abuse of children, given recent cases and the publicity around them. By far the greatest number of sex abuse cases, some 80 percent, involve people the children know well, not strangers who whisk them off the street, or teachers (though teachers from nursery schools and schools were involved in at least two of the more prominent recent cases). Much more common is abuse by a stepparent, a cousin, an aunt, an uncle, even a biological parent.

Instilling the awareness that private parts are indeed private can create a kind of warning system in your child, so that even if a trusted relative wants to touch them, your child will respond, "No, Mommy and Daddy told me no one is allowed to touch me there."

DEALING WITH DEATH

Children become interested in the idea of death around the age of five, and will start asking questions.

Simple explanations are best. "When people die, their bodies don't work anymore so they are put in the ground and they don't come back."

Add whatever religious context suits you. "They go to Heaven if they have been good."

When they ask if you will die: "Someday, but not for a long, long time. People don't usually die until they are very old."

Frequently, the death of a goldfish or other pet is a child's first experience with death.

Be honest. The pet is gone. Don't try to soften the truth with some tale of how Goldie has gone on a long, long trip. That will raise unanswerable questions in your child's mind. She can accept the basic facts: that Goldie lived a happy life, got sick, and now is dead. You can expect that she will have fantasies connected with Goldie's demise, fantasies of mutilation and disintegration, and thoughts that she somehow killed the fish.

Some friends of mine faced the common situation of having to put their dog to sleep. She was old and sickly, and repeated trips to the vet confirmed that she was sinking. After each visit to the vet, they made a point of telling their sons—aged six and three, and much in love with the dog—that things were getting worse. Before long, the older boy began talking about how Ginger was dying and asking if they could get another dog as soon as Ginger was gone.

When they knew for sure that the time had come to end Ginger's life, they made a special plan with the vet. With much warning, they took Ginger to the vet, telling the boys that this might be it. The vet was going to try the last medicine he knew. Over the next two days, they gave the boys increasingly bleak vet reports. Finally, they announced that the vet didn't think poor Ginger had long to live.

So they all went to the vet's to say good-bye for the last time. One boy took a piece of Ginger's favorite cheese, the other took one of her chew sticks. They all gave her their farewell gifts, their last hugs and kisses.

The next morning, the parents told their boys that the vet had called with the sad news: Ginger had died during the night. The six-year-old cried; the three-year-old kept playing with his barnyard animals. Ginger would be buried upstate, the parents explained, where dogs from New York City were buried.

For a couple of days, the older boy asked questions

about just how old Ginger had been, how all those years corresponded to human years. Both boys told everyone they saw that poor old Ginger had finally died.

And serious discussion started for everyone on the kind of dog they would all like to get to replace Ginger.

FUNERALS

I am often asked whether a five-year-old should be taken to a funeral. My answer is positively yes, but you should watch out for a few things.

I would not expose a child to an open casket, and I would not take her to the actual burial.

The sight of her dead grandpa in a casket will be too scary and confusing to her. If she's been told that grandpa is gone, he should be gone.

The actual burial, placing the casket into the ground, is often a time when you and other adults lose control. To see you that way is very disturbing to your child at any time.

Still, the funeral service itself can be meaningful for your child. Grandpa is dead and going away and something special is being done about it. This can help to relieve a common guilt fantasy: that she had something to do with Grandpa's death.

It becomes a landmark for her, even if she doesn't understand it all. Later in life, she will refer to it. It was the last time, in a sense, she had contact with Grandpa. That's much much better than a mysterious disappearance followed by a lot of puzzling crying on your part. Or a situation that leads to angry questions years later, especially if there was a close relationship between her and Grandpa. "Why didn't you ever give me a chance to say good-bye to Grandpa? . . . I think that was very unfair of you." The funeral can also prevent a fear from surfacing in her, a confusing fantasy that Grandpa was buried alive, which might have evolved if she had not attended the funeral but had merely been told that Grandpa had died and was buried.

It will also help you and her get through your period of mourning, which is difficult and confusing for her.

Mourning

She will tend to mistake mourning in you for anger. To her, you suddenly appear preoccupied and in a terrible mood. Children don't understand this and are frightened by it. Without any explanation, they have lost the presence and attention of a parent. She will fantasize that she has been bad and caused you to withdraw from her, perhaps that she is going to be sent away, like Grandpa was.

If, however, she was at the funeral and shared in that ritual good-bye to Grandpa, your father, you can explain to her that you aren't at all angry with her, but you're very sad because Grandpa is dead and you won't ever see him again. The funeral gives her something concrete to relate to.

Just as children don't understand mourning, parents don't understand that children mourn in a very different manner.

They don't sustain a sadness for days or weeks. Death is not lasting for them under the age of six. They feel sad for a minute or two, but sadness is an intolerable feeling for them, so they dispel it quickly and go off to play. It disturbs parents to see such a response, such apparent indifference.

Also, at first, your child might be irritating, asking day after day, "What happened to Grandpa?" or "Why are you sad?" or "Why is Daddy grumpy?" And you should try to keep explaining that Grandpa has gone and that you're not angry at her, or that Dad is not grumpy because of her.

Then, after that first period, children have a way of spreading out their mourning over three or four years. They will come back to it maybe a year later when they ask you, "Mommy, whatever happened to Grandpa? It's been so long since I've seen him." When you remind them of Grandpa's funeral, they will recollect and be sad for five minutes, then go off to play again.

There are times when people are dying and children get shunted aside in the chaos, and that can understandably be terrifying to them.

I think of the case where Grandpa, who lived with the family and was very close to his grandson, was hit by a car in the street right out in front of the family home.

For days he hung on, barely alive, in the hospital, and the family collapsed. The mother kept a continual vigil by her father's bedside, and a neighbor was asked to look after the five-year-old boy. The father, instead of giving extra time to his son, denied the events by going to work as usual.

The child really couldn't comprehend what had happened to his grandfather, to his world. All he knew was that everything had shattered overnight. His fantasy was that his whole world was coming apart.

He responded to the crisis with a panic of his own, his way of calling attention to the fact that he was terrified. Normally well behaved in school, he became a monster. He began pushing everybody around, and when one of his victims cut her lip on a desk, first the pediatrician, then I, was called in.

It didn't take long to figure out what had happened within the family and to the boy. In my first talk with the mother, she as much as said it, between her tears. "My father's dying in the hospital," she said to me, "and my child is having a breakdown, and I can't spend the time with him."

But she and her husband could see that they had to mobilize themselves. He had to take a couple of days off from work to walk his son to school and spend more time with him. They couldn't abandon him to a stranger. And as awful as the moment was, she had to resume being a mother again and bring a degree of normalcy back into their home.

They both responded, and very quickly the little boy calmed down. Life was back together again for him, and even when Grandpa died, which was not long after, the parents were now sensitive enough to their child not to push him aside in their grief.

6

The Age of Early Independence

(60 to 72 months)

The door to society opens wider, much wider, during this period, and your child will look in and take his first steps through it. He is making the major transition between absolute childhood and larger society.

He is no longer totally immersed in his own needs. Instead he's venturing, learning what it's like to be a member of the adult society where Mommy and Daddy live and work.

Erikson called it "the era of initiative," when the child is finding out what he can do to manipulate his world.

He begins to look more like an adult—in a smaller, simpler version—and wants very much to identify with Mommy and/or Daddy and imitate them. He wants to conquer the world, as they do, share adult aspirations, and work as they do. School is his place of business, where he goes off in the morning just as Daddy and, increasingly, Mommy go off to their offices. And by this time in most middle-class families he understands that a major goal in life is to do well in school, to excel, if he is going to win pleasure from his parents.

This expansion of himself and his world brings new possibilities with peers. New, deeper levels of friendships evolve. He begins to share and really play with other children, rather than simply playing in the same room with them and acknowledging their presence but not involving them.

The earlier seeds of rules and regulations begin to grow, and more formal ones come from you and his teachers. As a little member of society, he is expected to behave when guests appear or when the family goes to a restaurant.

Identification with parents is strong, usually with the parent of the same sex. Girls begin to be imitative of their mothers and boys of their fathers. The connection allows parents and society to hold a powerful influence over children, an influence that's applied directly and indirectly.

This is especially so when it comes to aspirations. Parents—and teachers, too, who are also influential societal figures at this time—subtly indicate what they would like to see a child become or not become.

Girls, especially, at around the age of five commonly receive indirect yet clear messages from their mothers that, for example, it's not such a great thing to think about becoming a firewoman, or policewoman, or girl lumberjack. They will also acquire the feeling that being a mommy is a great thing, and depending on the actual mommy's view, whether being a mommy and also working in a job is a good thing.

Children understand much more than parents realize they understand. They are always watching us, always aware of what we say, how we act, even when we forget they are around. This doesn't mean you should start looking over your shoulder all the time, but you should realize that your casual remark can have an effect on your child who happens to hear it: a biased remark, a statement criticizing a friend or a public figure, reaches deep. And to a child whose thinking is very concrete, when you say in frustration, "God, I wish I never had to go into that office again," you can conceivably affect her whole vision of work. This sensibility of theirs, these antennae, are defenses of sorts: it makes them not so easy to fool. You might say, "A doctor is a great thing to be." Yet, he understands something else: Then how come you're not a doctor, if it's so wonderful?

In terms of influencing them, it is easier for you to convey your lack of approval than it is to affect their thinking positively. In a way, they haven't changed. They always have been concerned about your displeasure. Now they are more responsive to what you disapprove of than what you approve of.

So a caustic remark that slips out about women as cops has a greater effect than your somewhat transparent statement about aspiring to the medical profession, although that will also register.

A friend told me about watching the 1984 Olympics with his wife and five-year-old daughter. They especially wanted her to see the women participants in swimming and gymnastics, two sports in which the girl showed some talent and interest. They also watched a number of the other events, including the women's marathon. When they saw the Swiss woman stagger into the stadium and practically collapse as she stumbled in total exhaustion around the track, the father pitied the woman and his wife cheered her on. Later he wondered about the effect of those comments. My guess is that the message their daughter picked up was that, it's okay to try to be an Olympic runner and to test the limits of your strength.

But you can see how my friend and his wife might have conveyed inadvertently a quite different message to the little girl if they had said: "What's wrong with that foolish woman? Doesn't she know when to stop?" In her mind she would translate that response to mean "Athletics are stupid and dangerous for a girl."

There is another kind of more positive influence for parents to make. Find out where your child's talents lie, and encourage him to develop them. During this age of initiative, his strengths will start to reveal themselves.

Many parents get unduly worried about some of the implications of what they see. Their boy seems to have talent as a painter, for example. Yet, life as a painter can be so difficult. Should they encourage him? I say, certainly, but if they are, even at his young age, worried about their son's starving in a garret, they don't have to overemphasize those skills.

Whatever direction you want to encourage, go easy. You could be planting the seeds now for a terrible power struggle between you and him later on. Some parents lose control of themselves in this area and they smother all signs of independence. They are so certain they know what's best, and so determined to impose their will, that they create a profound battle with no winners.

I remember a fellow who grew up with me whose father wanted nothing in life but for his son to become a doctor. The force of that desire was so great that the boy could never seem to bring himself to say no directly to his father. So he did it indirectly.

At college, he was a premed student, like me, but in his last year he deliberately failed three science courses so he would not be accepted at medical school. He was very bright, and at the time I was puzzled by what happened. Later, I realized that this desperate act was the only way he could deal with his father's suffocating desire.

During this stage, you should be able to get a clear picture of your child's sexual identity. As we discussed earlier, this is their sense of sexual being, and we see it manifested in the way a child dresses and acts.

Does your son dress and act like a boy, identify with being a male? Does your daughter clearly see herself as a female? Or is there confusion, and if so what does it mean and what can be done about it?

This whole area is unsettled and controversial today, and although there are treatments for homosexuality and transsexuality that sometimes work, there is a great deal that is not known about how and why these conditions develop.

There doesn't seem to be much question that a high proportion of effeminate boys at five and six turn out to be homosexual later in life. But not all of them do, and no one yet has been able to identify which little boys will become adult homosexuals and which won't.

When it comes to the causes of male homosexuality, there are often patterns of especially close relationships with mothers, of very protective mothers, of a corresponding lack of (or exclusion of) fathers as a strong influence, and of very hostile fathers. The result is a strong sense of identification by the young male with his mother and a rejection of maleness.

But there is also serious research being done on the biological basis of homosexuality, the possibility that there might be something subtle in the brain or the hormones that causes it. I remain open and uncertain myself.

In some ways, cross-dressing children who are bound and determined to be the other sex are more alarming than effeminate boys. This is the beginning of transvestism, most commonly boys wearing dresses and insisting they want to be girls, and it is usually the sign of some serious confusion on the part of the child and should be treated.

For boys this usually stems from a peculiarly intense relationship between the boy and his mother, which has existed since birth and has cut his father out. A real and fantasized unity evolves with the parent of the opposite sex.

That's with boys. With girls, something else that isn't clear to us develops. If you take a large group of transsexual women, females who want to be males, you won't find the same sense of intimacy between them and their fathers. What has happened to them is part of continuing research on this tough subject.

Milder confusions about sexual identity at this age can be more easily treated. I had a case with rather typical elements not long ago, a boy of five and a half who wasn't sure whether he wanted to be a boy or a girl. He dressed in girls' clothes much of the time, played with dolls, identified with Batgirl and Wonder Woman.

His mother had not nurtured the kind of intense closeness between them I have found in other cases, but she had unconsciously encouraged his effeminate tendencies. She let him play with female clothes and told him how cute he was while he was doing it. In addition, she bought him girls' toys and dolls. The child was dealing with conscious and unconscious fantasies that being female was more rewarding than being male.

Meanwhile, the boy's father also contributed unconsciously by seeing very little of him. A kind of workaholic, he came home after the boy went to bed, often left the house in such a rush in the morning that he barely had time to say more than hello to his son, and he never did anything with him.

Fortunately, I could get the parents to understand what had been happening and to try to change. The mother stopped being a positive reinforcer of nonmasculine behavior. The father entered his son's life. He made time for him in the morning and at night, began to play with him and take him places. He became the male model the boy needed.

Meanwhile, I worked with the boy in therapy, and after some six months of effort from all of us, we could see a quite dramatic change. He began to drop the transvestite behaviors and showed a masculine identification. Among other changes, he started to play with little boys. Up to then, he had only one friend, a little girl.

Fortunately, with that boy there was a kind of opening to begin with, in that he was uncertain what he wanted to be. In another case, a six-year-old boy came in who was absolutely committed to being a girl, and he had been since he was two and a half.

A dramatically disturbing event happened in his life at that age and it reshaped his whole sexual orientation. He lost his parents, or so it appeared to him.

His younger sister had fallen critically ill and had been hospitalized for five months. For that period, he was dumped at his grandmother's, barely seeing his parents. In his own primitive fantasies, he decided several things: his parents were gone; he was a boy, and his sister, who was getting all their time, love, and attention, was a girl; therefore it was better to be a girl.

He didn't cross-dress, but all his mannerisms from the time he was two and a half were imitative of his mother and sister. The fact that his father was away much of the time and not greatly involved with his son added to the boy's turn of mind.

This family decided to put him into a therapy program at a nearby hospital that was studying such sexual disorders, a major program that cost them next to nothing.

My prognosis at the time was not very optimistic. The boy was very committed to being a girl, and like so many youngsters with his characteristics, he has remained that way.

What happened here might seem extreme, but one aspect of it is quite commonplace and needs to be watched. There was an emergency in the family. The parents put other priorities before their child's, and that had, and could have in other circumstances, a profound effect on the little boy. All he knew was that he had suffered an abrupt, profound loss. His attempt to understand why led him to respond in a radical way. If you should be faced with a similar crisis, try to remember your other children.

A NEW KIND OF HIGH-QUALITY TIME

I haven't mentioned high-quality time for a while, but I think you can see that the nature of it changes as your child grows and changes.

At this stage, the games you play with her will involve elements of skill as well as chance. Dominoes, simple word and memory games, card games such as Go Fish! and War!, possibly checkers.

She is ready to learn something from you about losing. Up to now, remember, she simply couldn't accept losing. But now, if you lose to her, perhaps a bit more than you win, and point out to her that even though she beat you you're not getting upset, that you're still able to enjoy the game, she'll start to get the message. You can convey to her that there is such a thing as a "good loser."

She is also ready now to share "adult" activities with you. They might be simple events, but very special to her.

You might take her to a restaurant, for example. It could—in fact, should—be a simple neighborhood place or a fast-food place, not your favorite three-star French restaurant. For her it will be a real occasion.

Going to the movies, or even to the theater, is another treat for her—assuming, of course, you pick the right one. Nothing too scary at the movies and probably a musical on the stage. Remember, Walt Disney built an empire on movies for children of this age for good reasons. If she is beginning to show an interest in music and dance, you might even try a ballet. *The Nutcracker* is a Christmas favorite, danced by companies all over the country and adored by children at this age. The circus, of course, is intended for children of all ages, and it can be captivating.

Shopping for clothes begins to assume new meaning

for her. She's no longer just making the trip with you; now she should be involved in decisions. There are limits, obviously, but the more she can decide between, say, a red shirt and a blue one, the better. She's ready to exercise judgment and assume that sort of responsibility.

INCREASING RESPONSIBILITY

This is a time when your child can begin to take on responsibilities around the house in a modest way.

He's not able to do much during the first three to four years. But you should avoid doing everything for him, because you begin to teach him that he doesn't have to do anything, or that he isn't capable of doing anything. So, increasingly he tries to fix his toy or put his shoes on the right feet, and you let him struggle. If he can't manage, you suggest that maybe the two of you can do it together.

Now, he might well volunteer to be your helper. Encourage him. Let him help with particular chores. He can imitate you taking out the garbage, or even better, cleaning up his own room.

Messy rooms become the source of so many battles in later years that you might well spare yourself by sharing the picking up process with him.

Helping you is also a route to the allowance, which often begins at the end of this period. An allowance is a great tool. He earns it by assuming some specific responsibilities, such as helping to clean up his room or clearing his own dishes from the table.

OVERBOOKING ACTIVITIES

As your child steps into society, there are a number of new activities and opportunities for her. Try to keep them under control.

It's quite a range. You might want to start taking her

to church or temple. There may be a story program at your local library that sounds good. The Y may have a ceramics class and you might have heard of a dancing teacher who's great with children.

Test and choose. Not everything has to be done at once. I run into this fairly often, when I'm called in for a consultation on a child. After a couple of exploratory sessions, I tell the parents that we should try to schedule a regular hour for therapy for a while. However, I quickly discover that it's practically impossible to find a free hour,- that from eight in the morning to six at night every day that child is simply programmed to death.

Establish a hierarchy of what you really feel she ought to be involved with now and what can be put off.

RELIGIOUS TRAINING

This is one of those new activities that won't wait, assuming you are serious about getting a religious education for your child.

As we discussed early in the book, if yours is a mixed marriage, the whole question of how much religious education for your child, and what kind, hopefully was settled before he was born.

If you're both of the same religion, long before now you should have agreed on how much training you want for him.

One important caution: if you want him to accept religious education, you have to be involved in some kind of religious activity yourself.

This is not one of those areas where you can say, do as I say, not as I do, and have the best results.

If you are completely nonobservant, indifferent, or atheistic, you're developing a potentially strong conflict within your child. Why should he go to Sunday school if you don't believe and support what he's being taught?

Frequently, as children grow older, they resent spending time at this extra school. They would much rather spend Sundays with their friends. In the Jewish religion, Hebrew school is a weekday program, taking up afternoons they might well prefer to spend playing sports.

I've seen countless conflicts around this with children between ten and fifteen, resentful that they are being forced to go through the religious process when they can see that it means so little to their parents.

If you want your child to receive a religious education, be a good model for him. If you have theological doubts, but still feel that religious education ought to be part of this general cultural and educational experience, then make a special effort to include the religious in your own cultural life. At least share the holidays with him, attend those services together. Show an interest in what he is learning in religious school. Let him see and feel that you do care that he is exposed to this educational and moral process.

ONLY CHILDREN

If yours is an only child, you might find her having imaginary conversations with invisible companions or favorite stuffed bears and dolls.

This is merely an extension of the animalism of an earlier age. (This part of your child's fantasy world can be just as attractive to adults. Witness the popularity of Winnie-the-Pooh, Linus and his blanket, Calvin and Hobbes.) It's nothing at all to worry about, assuming she relates to other children and functions satisfactorily in school.

There is a certain amount of discussion about whether or not it's good to have only one child. It can be terrific, and certainly there's nothing wrong with it.

Obviously, it's no good if you spoil an only child in such a way that you create a difficult, lazy person.

Doing everything, providing everything, for any child

is dangerous. Freud wisely observed that normality in life requires two elements: love and work. If you do everything for her, you are eliminating the concept of work.

It also subtly transmits an extremely destructive message to her: you're incapable of doing anything for yourself, incapable of really functioning. I see that communicated by parents who have no idea they're doing it. Indeed, they think they are being all-caring, all-loving, all-wonderful parents.

On the other hand, spoiling can take quite positive forms. It can mean that you lavish the best education money can buy on your one child, which you might not be able to do if you had four or five educations to buy.

It can mean that you spoil her with plenty of quality time, not having to split yourself and your energies with any siblings.

Indeed, there is data that only children tend to be somewhat more ambitious and brighter, or at least more curious and intellectually tuned, than children with siblings, who can get somewhat lost in the pack.

However, there are also a number of desirable qualities we see in children from large families. They tend to have a greater ability to share, for example. And they are more responsible. Also, they are less self-centered; only children tend to be self-important.

Is there an ideal family size? Not that I know of.

SEXUAL ABUSE

By this age, you should have gotten the message across to your child that his private parts are just that, and except for an occasional examination by the doctor, no stranger should be touching him there.

It's a message best conveyed by a number of calm repetitions, without alarm.

As I noted earlier, you should listen to your child as

he talks about events at school and his life at large and take him seriously.

If he starts talking about physical abuse—or about being fondled, touched, played with—you'll know he's not fantasizing. He will describe what happened in realistic, concrete terms. He will be detailed. When he tells you about such an experience, assume it's real until you can satisfy yourself that it's otherwise.

As for warning about such dangers, try to be balanced. Certainly, such a warning is important. But you want a calm, reasoned attitude toward sexuality in the first place. You can't very well present that and then frighten him to death, exhorting him that people are going to be waiting to rape and assault him every time he walks out the door, and this at a time when he's beginning to understand the difference between his own fantasy life and reality.

Your best defenses are to look closely at his school and the people teaching there before you put him in it, and then to listen to him and believe him.

Trust is important for this kind of communication. He'll come to you quickly when something is wrong if he thinks you'll take him seriously. I suspect that in some of the recent abuse cases children kept news of what was going on to themselves because of fear of how their parents would respond to them.

THE NO-PLAY, NO-FUN CHILD

There are children who are all business. They really don't know how to play or have fun. Intense, driven to succeed at school, they seem years and years older than they actually are.

These are obsessive-compulsive children, and I treat many of them. They are frequently the children of successful, professional parents.

Though it's possible for such a child to acquire some of this high intensity from temperament, it's clear that the model of the parents and the way they live affects him directly.

These children identify strongly with their parents, who most often are not openly, consciously trying to mold their child into any sort of superachiever. Yet, that's the message the child receives, even when the parents bring him to me for help because they themselves feel their child is not being a child, is not having any fun.

Indeed, what I usually find is that the child doesn't know how to play. There has not been much time given to playing in his young life, and that is partly the fault of parents who have overprogrammed him, nurtured the idea that play comes after all our work is done. For these children, however, work seems never to be done. There is usually a great lack of quality playtime; in fact, the parents simply don't play with their child.

In therapy with these children and their parents, I can't very well tell them to cut down on the amount of success around the house. But I can try to get them to make some adjustments in their life-styles to allow for more high-quality time with the child. I also advise them to see that there are periods reserved simply for games and playing, and more social outlets, playing with other children. I try to get the idea across that there are other ways in life to succeed besides getting all A's in school. I try to teach them to relax.

These children will always have a drive to succeed, which obviously is not bad, but they might also be able to moderate the intensity of that drive and the subtle unhappiness it seems to generate. They might be able to accept life's inevitable failures without feeling that each is a hopeless disaster, and shake the feeling that life is always so ominous or ponderous.

COMPUTERS

Back when television was becoming an accepted part of every home, I recall being interviewed on the goods and evils of TV for children. These days, the interviews concern home computers.

The two are not dissimilar in that you should exercise control over the use of a computer by your child, as you should over the viewing of TV, which we've discussed.

It does clearly appear that in the coming five to ten years computers will be ever more broadly used in our society, becoming everyday tools in our lives.

A real computer is far better for your child than something that hooks up to the TV set for video games. With a grown-up computer, there are a number of programs designed for reading and learning skills, drawing, making up tunes, all of which can become part of your child's whole educational development. But the video games are repetitive, on the whole rather mindless and expensive.

TOOLS, TOYS, BRIBES, VALUES

We are surrounded by "things" in our consumer society, and I have found a widespread concern in parents over having their children drowned in them, having their relationships with their children distorted by them, having the values of their children warped by them.

There are distinctions we ought to make here.

First, some of these things, such as cars, are tools. We must use them to make everyday life efficient. Where appropriate, we encourage our children to use them. Spoons, forks, and toilets are such tools. Computers will become such tools.

Then there are tools for entertainment, or toys. The TV is a prime example.

The use of things for materialistic bribes is something

else, an insidious element in your relationship with your child.

As we discussed earlier, don't substitute things for love, don't make a material thing the symbol of your love. That's called conditional love: "You do X, and I'll give you Y."

At the same time, we know that rewards are a useful part of teaching a child, helping a child to develop along particular lines. But these rewards can be measured, as we saw with the gold star system. An allowance at this point might be appropriate as a kind of parallel to a salary in the outer grown-up world. The effect of that kind of materialistic reinforcement is an early and natural introduction to the work ethic, which is something I believe parents ought to teach: You have to put in work for a while before you get either a concrete reward or a loving reward.

Materialistic rewards are by no means the only ones you should be giving. There are hugs and kisses and elaborate thanks and expressions of love, all for trying to do something, whether it worked or not.

There is the special, sudden playtime. "I'm so happy you did that, let's have a special game of checkers, right now." Or "You've been so good, let's drop everything and take a walk in the park."

One of the ways to balance the materialistic flood, then, is to change the currency. Instead of things being the rewards all the time, make yourself and your time and your love the rewards.

7

Special Conditions

I'd like to conclude the book by addressing four potentially difficult issues that a family might face: sibling rivalry, adoption, divorce, and serious illness and hospitalization of the child. Each of these developments can profoundly affect your child in her first six years and each requires intelligent and sensitive handling on your part as a parent.

SIBLING RIVALRY

One of the best ways of grasping the dynamics of the rivalry that explodes between your older child and your younger one is to look at life for a moment from the perspective of the older one.

There she is at, say, age three, having enjoyed three years at the center of the world. The world revolved around her. She did not have to share your attention or your husband's affection with anyone.

Further, she has recently gone through a rough stage where she has given up certain pleasures in order to please you. She has learned to exercise control and use a toilet.

Now, all of a sudden, there is this other creature who is noisily demanding your time and love.

To make matters worse, she is now being pushed out of the house, sent off to pre-nursery school.

In her mind, getting her out of the way will let you and Daddy have all day to play with the baby. And who knows where this will lead? Maybe this is only the beginning. Maybe you and Daddy will forget her completely, stop taking care of her, stop feeding and clothing her.

Looked at that way, it's not hard to understand your older child's resentment. Life has dealt her a mean, unfair blow.

She might well respond to this threat by regressing. Quite naturally she might get the idea that if she returns to her earlier form of behavior—acting, in fact, the way this new organism is acting—life might return to normal. I had a case of a little girl who started walking around with her baby bottle again, though she had given it up six months before. And every time her mother began to breast-feed the new baby, the older child wanted the other breast.

There are some steps you can take to minimize these problems, and they begin with pregnancy and delivery.

As soon as you know you are pregnant and everyone is jumping for joy, share the news with your first child. A new baby is growing in Mommy's tummy and in nine months you will have a new brother or sister. (Do not, by the way, be concerned about getting into a detailed discussion of sex and reproduction with your innocent child. She will not yet be asking those questions.)

Prepare her and involve her as much as possible. When it comes time for you to go into the hospital, explain that the time has arrived when the baby wants to come out of Mommy's tummy. Be sure she knows where you are going, for how long, and how soon she can talk to you on the phone and come and visit you and her new brother or sister. If your hospital doesn't permit infants to visit, tell her that.

She will be needy at this time. Above all, avoid the catastrophic behavior I have seen on occasion when parents have dumped the first child with a neighbor or relative for several days, the father barely seeing her, the mother disappearing.

If possible, let her stay at home in her own familiar environment with plenty of extra time with her father.

Once the baby is home, let the older child be Mother's helper. Maybe she can, with your supervision, help powder the baby, even if that means that a lot of powder ends up all over the floor.

If the baby's arrival does coincide with the older child's going off to pre-nursery school, try to make that seem like something special. It won't be easy, but convey the idea that rather than this being a banishment, it is a great reward. Older children get to go to this place where there are wonderful new games, stories, paints, and plenty of other older children to play with.

As both children grow a bit older, establish the notion that age has its privileges. She gets to stay up later than her brother, for example, and during that extra half hour she gets a story read to her by Mommy or Daddy.

Don't twin the two. I've seen numerous cases in which much of the trouble between siblings evolves from this, parents treating the two children just the same. Instead, allow the older one to stay up later, perhaps go to special places where the baby can't go, do special things, maybe eat special treats.

Further along, there will be other potential problems.

The hand-me-down problem, for example. It is only natural that the baby ends up being clothed in much of the stuff that the older sibling wore, all the more so if they are the same sex. Just be careful that not everything is a hand-me-down. Balance things out. Otherwise, a profound resentment on the part of the younger child can develop, and not surprisingly.

I'm often asked about siblings of different sexes sharing baths. In the early years, there's no problem with that. When one reaches five, the other seven, you'll want to separate them and it can be done by simply stating, "You're too big to have a bath with your brother. Time for you to have a bath all your own."

Another common question is whether they should go to the same school. Generally, it doesn't matter if they are comparable children. If one has problems, is slow to learn, and is constantly comparing himself to his sister, then he should probably go to a new school.

I would be especially careful with twins. Make sure they have different teachers so that they are not always being compared and encouraged to compete.

For all your efforts, I think you can see how naturally your older child will develop resentment toward the new baby. At times this can result in truly aggressive feelings and actions on the part of the older one, and you should be alert to that.

Be firm. If you see the older one pushing her little brother around, taking his toys from him, make it clear by your tone and face that this is dangerous behavior. If she persists and that same day repeats the action, punish her verbally. On the third strike, take something away from her. She is not going to be allowed to play with her favorite doll.

Explain to her: "If you are upset with your baby brother, you can yell at him, but you are not allowed to push him or hit him."

If a couple of hours go by after such an incident and all is well, let her know how pleased you are. "You know you've been very grown up. You have stopped pushing Andrew." And give her a big hug.

As dangerous as this aggressive behavior might be, watch out for one common trap. If you don't see it, don't punish it. When the younger child is able to verbally complain, at about two and a half, he might well start blaming everything on his older sibling. It's a great way for him to get your attention and affection, he thinks.

Don't fall for it, or you develop a small agent provocateur. You will be encouraging the little one to continuously complain, and the big one will grow increasingly furious at the little one for always being blamed.

If there is evidence that something has happened, you might want to punish both children equally. Otherwise, assume that you do not really know. Often an admonition to both is sufficient: "Whatever happened, stop it. You two work it out."

Is there an ideal spacing of years between your children? It's hard to say. There is one school that contends that it's best to have them in rapid succession.

I think that it is better if there are three to four years between them. Then the older one has adequate language, can talk and comprehend so much more. You can explain what is happening. You have a much better chance of talking and working with that child around the issues of jealousy and resentment. If the children come right after each other, the older one hasn't yet developed adequate language or the beginnings of a rational mind. She is still such a baby herself that she is more likely to resent the second child and be unable to integrate what it means to have a brother or sister.

Working parents who have to ration their time with their children should give this real thought. If there are two babies close together, there will be two equally demanding babies. If they are separated in years, you can better balance their needs and your time with them.

ADOPTION

In some ways, raising an adopted child is even more demanding than raising your own infant.

To begin with, these children require a great deal more trust of their adoptive parents, so that everyone can handle the inevitable shock to come: telling the child that he or she is adopted.

To the child, that means she was rejected by her natural parents, a complex and tough psychological burden. So even though you might not tell her what has happened until she is three or four, when she can comprehend your message, from the beginning you have to develop something special with your child.

One of the things this means is that one parent, usually the mother, should not return to work after some three months, as I recommended for natural mothers who work, but rather stay at home with the baby pretty much through the first year. That additional contact will nurture the closer, warmer, more trusting relationship that will be needed later on.

There are other reasons for such a special effort. One of these is that you didn't go through a pregnancy. That nine months helps to prepare you psychologically for your new role. It also focuses you and your husband on the changes you both are going to make in your lives. Unfortunately, there is no substitute for that pregnancy experience.

I always counsel couples who come to me considering adoption to do all the talking and thinking they can. Good adoption agencies run group sessions that are helpful. Find couples who have adopted and have your own sessions with them. Read books on the subject.

All of that helps to prepare you, but it is never enough. The extra time at home with the adopted baby, however, can make a great difference. In a way, you'll be catching up on the job, but my experience is that it very much helps parents and baby in the huge adjustment.

Match and Mismatch

These days, if you are Caucasian and go to an agency, you have practically no chance of being matched with a Caucasian child. There is an active gray market of Caucasian children coming from South America, but if the agency can provide you with any child, that child is likely to be Black, Hispanic, or Oriental.

Any such child might be absolutely wonderful, but the fact is that you will have a problem adjusting to a child who does not resemble you and/or your husband. The child will not match your fantasies. The flaws in this child will be tougher to accept. You might accept the same things easily in your own child, but not so readily in someone else's—and that the child is someone else's is reinforced by the differences in looks.

The child might also be different temperamentally and intellectually from you and your husband. "Temperamental mismatches" are a big problem with adoptions, and a number of them end up in my office.

I had one child who was born to be a professor and by chance ended up in a very athletic family that put little stress on intellectual achievement. They brought him to me when he was about three and a half because they thought he was growing up homosexual. It was kind of classic. The child was effete, and the fact that he came out of the black market from two hippie parents worried the adoptive parents greatly. At three and a half, he was practically reading. His parents wanted him to go out and play, and he wanted to sit and read.

Everyone had to adjust to the difference of temperaments in this reconstructed family, which they more or less did. And the boy thrived. Today he is a brilliant young man, on his way to being, I'm sure, a successful scientist.

These mismatches do not always end so happily. I've seen innumerable cases in which the child with some temperamental limitations simply cannot get along with his new family—a very passive child, for example, in a high-energy, driven, type-A family. This is often the case with professional families.

Or consider the intellectually normal child in a brilliant family. The odds are that an adopted child will have an average IQ and be an average child. Yet, so often I see these children pushed far beyond their limits. They are placed in schools that are far too competitive for them and they end up getting C's and D's. By the time they're eight they're functioning badly, depressed, possess a low self-esteem, and are in trouble in school. Beyond which, they're in a school where the average IQ is 125 and they score at 100. They push themselves so hard, pursuing irrational goals, that they burn themselves out by eight or ten.

Earlier, I spoke of the need for one of the adopting parents to stay home longer with the baby. Many of the problems we're considering are not going to reveal themselves immediately. It's a good idea for you to be aware of them and to be there if and when they do start to appear.

I don't mean to unduly scare a couple that's thinking about adoption. But these additional adjustment problems are realities. They require a very strong commitment from both parents, and ironically, something of an extra parental effort.

The Surprise Sibling

No one has yet explained it, but over and over again a couple will adopt a child and a few months later will discover that the mother is pregnant. Something at a very deep psychological level could have prevented fertility from functioning properly, and the impact of adoption released it.

That mystery phenomenon might bring joy to the parents, but not to their adopted child. He needs undivided attention for about a year, and an instant sibling is going to disturb him. He'd probably be better off if he were an only child for two years.

His reactions can be dealt with, of course, but that's another reason for the extended period of full-time parenting.

When to Tell a Child

In the best of all worlds, an adopted child would never know she was adopted. But you don't live in a vacuum in the real world, and if you don't tell your child, she will learn by a slip made by Grandma or Auntie or someone else, or will be confronted by the truth in some other sudden, painful way. So there is really no question of whether or not to tell your child.

There is no best way to do this, only the least worst. In other words, it is an extremely tough thing for you to explain and for your child to grasp and accept. The special, deeper trust you have built, it is hoped, by the time you sit down with her for that wrenching conversation will cushion the shock.

However difficult it is to tell her this, it is infinitely better and less harmful than having the child discover the truth for herself later on in life. That kind of accident can shred the relationship you have with her and affect her total functioning.

The best time to tell her is early, as soon as there is some reasonable communication between you.

I would start around the age of three, when she can begin to understand and ask some simple questions. She won't react much at first. She's not really sophisticated enough to absorb the whole idea of adoption. As she grows and her insight and understanding increase, her questions will become more complicated and your answers should be fuller and increasingly complex.

Handle it as you handle questions about pregnancy and birth. When the three-year-old asks where does Baby come from, you say from Mother. When she asks again at four, you say from a special place inside

Mother. Each time it comes up, your response should be more complex.

I have helped some families in which the child was not told, in which the parents thought they never would have to.

In one case, the family was European, had settled here intending never to return. People from their town in the old country knew they had adopted a son, but no one in America did. They intended never to tell him.

All went well for eight years, and then the mother's father fell seriously ill and the family had to go back to their old hometown. They came to me in a panic, but as soon as I saw the boy with his parents I was sure there would be little trouble. There was such love in that family.

At my suggestion, they explained to the boy that he was, in fact, adopted, and that obviously they loved him as if he were their own. They had never told him about the adoption because they thought he would be better off without knowing. But now they wanted to tell him rather than have him hear something from someone back in their old town.

The news, of course, was startling to the boy, but he handled it quite well. His bonds to his adopted parents were so strong, and their love for him was so deep, that he wasn't threatened. Though this was a profound and sudden twist in his life, his base was secure. These parents were never going to leave him.

They, incidentally, were enormously relieved. Though the matter of adoption had not come up for eight years, they had borne considerable anxiety about it during that time.

With the other case, the boy was five when his parents came to me under similar circumstances. They had lived and raised him near New York, and everyone in their family who knew about the adoption lived in Arizona. They also thought they could isolate him, and they too were now returning to the extended family and faced the possibility that someone would say something to him.

They were confused about what to say and how to say it. I suggested that they tell the boy that when the family got to Arizona someone might say something to him about being adopted. And it was true. They hadn't said anything to him before because they didn't think he was old enough to understand it. And certainly it didn't make any difference in the way they felt about him and loved him. But now he was a big boy and could understand it.

Those parents and their child also coped quite well, again because there was a strong sense of family among them, real trust and love.

DIVORCE

If a divorce is difficult for the adults going through it, it is worse for their children.

Children develop close bonds to both parents. To have those nurturing, protective ties shredded is terrifying to them. Half their little world is cut away. Normally, it is the worst form of separation they have yet experienced.

In my office, I see three kinds of divorce.

First and least malign are parents who have decided to split but have the sensitivity to recognize that the needs of their children come first. We are going to divorce, they say to me. What should we do for the children?

Second is more common, what I consider the standard, divorce. This is one in which there is a period of fighting—usually verbal, though there might be a thrown glass or two, loud damaging accusations, several slammed doors, people storming into the night, and tears. For somewhat older children, seven or eight, the fighting often signals the impending split. They are still left disturbed and anxious, but at least they are not caught completely by surprise.

In this divorce situation, the adults and children involved come to me some while after the divorce when
the children are showing signs of anxiety. Often it's
school trouble. They are no longer good learners, or
playing well with others. Their personalities have
changed completely, the parents tell me.

Quite typical was the little girl who had been gregar-
ious and happy and now had become a child who
wouldn't play and who spent most of her time depressed, crying, lonely, frightened. As I came to understand, not only had the child been frightened by the
loss of her father, but now she was terrified that she
was going to lose her mother as well. Indeed, the mother's response to the divorce, not uncommon, was one
of depression. So, in a foreboding way, the little girl
sensed the loss of both parents.

The third sort of divorce is the most destructive. This
is the highly contested custodial battle, sometimes even
involving kidnapping. I have never seen a child go
through such a war who isn't ravaged by it, left with
severe personality disorders. These sad children, vic-
timized by their profoundly angry parents, have trouble
with everybody and everything. They have trouble making relationships, trouble with authority and society.
They grow into very angry adolescents, failing out of
schools, falling into drugs or other antisocial activities.

How to Tell Them

The best way to tell children that a marriage and
home are breaking up is to be direct and honest, yet
supportive and loving, not an easy thing to accomplish.

When the time comes, both parents should sit down
with the children and say it. "Mommy and Daddy have
decided that Daddy's [Mommy's] going to leave. We
both love you, but we don't love each other and we
really can't live together anymore. It's not your fault.
Don't think it is. We both love you as much as ever.
And you'll see Daddy [Mommy] all the time. But he

isn't going to live here anymore. He's going to be living on the East Side.''

Once you've told them, it's best for Daddy, who usually does the moving, to do so quickly. If he stays around it will be confusing to a child. A three-year-old simply won't understand the ambiguity of going yet staying. His thinking is concrete. If Mommy and Daddy are separating, they're separating. Best to leave and quickly have the children bring some toys and come and visit, so they can see where Daddy is and that there's room for them in his new home.

A delayed leaving will also feed a three-year-old's likely, if misbegotten, response: I can bring them back together. In this Oedipal stage, the child imagines omnipotence, and so he'll make all this go away and make everything better.

His first response to the news will probably be, ''What did I do? How did I cause this?''

That can become a terrible burden for a little child, and his parents have to dispel it in two ways. They have to show him in word and deed that the divorce is not his fault. And they have to demonstrate repeatedly that whatever went on between them will not come between him and either of them.

One of the first things this means is that the parent who moves out must come back on a regular, frequent basis. The implicit message in having that continuous time together is: I told you it was not your fault. I told you I still love you, even if Mommy and I had our fights and stopped loving each other, even if I had to move out. Here we are, you and I, still together, still loving each other.

There has to be a great consistency in this new routine and ritual. The visits must be regular. If Daddy can't come, he should call and explain. And this should be sustained for two or three years at least. The younger the child at the time of the divorce, the longer the supportive, reassuring routine should continue. After that, there are other arrangements more suitable to the advancing age of the child. But by then he should have the solid proof he so desperately needs that, in fact, his father really does love him and the whole collapse of a universe was not his fault.

Mommy or Daddy?

Who should have primary custody of the child?

Up to the age of six, usually the mother.

I am aware of the current debate, and I have seen a number of fathers become primary caregivers of their children and raise them well.

But the greatest evidence is that the young child's primary caregiver, the parent the child has been closest to most of the time, where the bond is strongest, is the better single custodian. That normally is the mother.

Ideally, the parents will be able to agree on this and the complementing visitation arrangements and sit down and explain it all to the child.

The arrangements should allow an option when the child reaches seven or eight. Beyond that age, he might want to spend more time with his father, perhaps live with him for a year and get to know him better. So long as such a change isn't terribly disruptive to his education and social development, he should be able to do so.

I have seen a certain number of shared custody arrangements that have worked quite well for the children involved. They more or less alternate nights with their parents, and although there are certain logistical knots, the children come through such plans feeling that, indeed, whatever tore their parents apart, they both care as much about them as always.

The worst thing for a child under six is to be forced to make a choice, which is what frequently happens in court-custody cases. This is a hopelessly terrifying, difficult burden to be placed on a child.

The Angry Aftermath

Expect anger.

No matter how carefully sensitive parents try to handle and explain the divorce, children can be expected to go through a period of months, sometimes years, of anger.

They will vent their anger first on Mother, or the parent they're living with. That might hardly seem or be fair, but fairness has nothing to do with this.

Daddy, or the visiting parent, has an implicit threat over them: that he'll stop visiting. He's usually somewhat more intimidating anyway. So children will be on good behavior with him, and the blame they direct at Mommy will rise as they get more confident that Mommy is not also going to leave them.

It's a very, very tough business for a woman who is trying at the same time to deal with all her own feelings of anger, sadness, and insecurity, and making enormous adjustments in her life.

Children often assume at first that they are responsible for driving Daddy away, that they weren't good enough. Then they decide to blame their mothers for the split. It's easier on them. Often they directly accuse their mothers. "Why did you make Daddy go away? Why can't you make Daddy come home? When is Daddy going to come back and live with us?"

The poor mother must try to accept the child's anger without getting angry back. It's extremely trying, especially when a mother has to repeat a litany of explanations over and over because children this age don't retain things very well.

Sometimes children displace their feelings on their peers and start hitting everybody in their class. Or they get depressed and mope. Or they continue to believe that they have driven their father away. They say to him, "If I promise to be good—not like I was before—won't you come home?" Both parents have to try to dispel that talk and attitude by reinforcing their original message: "You're a good girl. It has nothing to do with you. It's just that Mommy and Daddy can't get along very well."

Consistency Over All

With the child swinging between them, the divorced parents have the difficult job of sustaining a consistency and evenness.

They can't undermine one another, even though their natural instincts might be to do just that. They are angry themselves, unhappy, guilty about their failure to make their marriage work. Even in the best of break-ups, the temptation to demean and disparage the other with the child is great. "Oh, your mother's being foolish to make you do that," is the kind of typical hostile statement that can leave the child less and less respectful of the parent.

We spoke of this need for consistency at various points earlier in the book. Without it, a child will manipulate his parents and destroy discipline and structure. This is never truer than in divorce.

What can easily happen (and frequently does) is that the divorced parents become competitive for the love of their child. One undermines the other; one tries to outdo the other.

If Dad takes her to a pizza place for dinner, Mom will take her the very next night to a real French restaurant. If Dad gives her a Barbie doll on her visit, Mom comes up with a whole dollhouse.

The temptation to do this is strong, especially with fathers who often have a related problem. So many of them are not accustomed to spending a whole weekend alone with their three-year-old. They don't really know how to play with the child. So what they tend to do is produce spectaculars: roller skating, then a movie, then a pizza, all in one day.

What the child needs is normalcy. Comfortable time playing with her father, getting to know him, doing what she would do on a regular day: some games, some Play-Doh, building a house with blocks, drawing pictures, and since it is the weekend, maybe a visit to the park if the weather is nice.

All that an overproduced visit does is excite and fatigue the child and certainly wear out the father. It doesn't contribute much to building the close, loving relationship they both need now more than ever.

Inadvertently, it also fuels the competition between parents. If he did all that, the mother says to herself, just watch what I'm going to do with her.

For other reasons, after the weekend visit with Dad, the child most likely will be upset for a few hours after returning home. She is reliving the pain of separation, and the custodial parent should expect a short period of difficulty and, for the sake of everyone, put up with it. It's another way of showing the child how much she is loved and cared for.

Often counseling is needed by the parents before they can understand and control their churning emotions. Normally, I'll work with each parent four to six times over as many weeks, then perhaps once every few weeks, and as things become smoother, once every three to six months. On some occasions parents are able to transcend their anger and work together in sessions with me. It's not an excessive amount of therapy, and it can make quite a difference for the parents and their children.

Dad's Special Role

If Dad drops away from his children after the divorce, there's trouble.

It's a terrible blow and rejection for the children to cope with, and it also belies the supportive statements you've made that it's not their fault.

If Dad rejects them, they will certainly feel it is their fault. For years they will carry the belief that if only they had been better in some way, he would not have gone away.

His disappearance also removes the preeminent male model in their lives. He has been that from the beginning of their lives, of course, but from the time the children were two, his role has grown increasingly significant. It's possible for children to have other males as models—a grandfather, an uncle, Mom's new boyfriend. But if humanly possible until the children are at least twelve, the father should try to sustain a relationship with them, in which he is still their primary male authority figure. Desertion at any age is harmful, but beyond twelve, a child's ability to integrate other male figures into his life becomes greater, so a loss then might not be quite such a blow.

Both boys and girls need a significant male model, especially at younger ages. Without a positive male relationship in their lives, children are more likely to develop problems relating to males. Boys may have more difficulties relating at first to male authority figures, and perhaps also to their peers. And they may have some difficulties learning to function heterosexually. That does not mean a boy who does not see his divorced father will necessarily become a homosexual, but as he grows up he probably will experience more difficulties in learning to relate to women.

Girls can be similarly affected. Rejected by the transcendent man in their lives, abandoned by and stripped of the familiar male figure as they grow up, they can have problems relating to other males later in life.

Replacing the male model can be difficult these days. In the past, an uncle was nearby, already a part of the extended family. It is tougher today; families are scattered, less cohesive. Many children compensate by substituting a favorite male teacher.

The Alimony Weapon

A boy who was almost three was brought to me by his mother. He was suffering night terrors, night after night.

The reason was so apparent even his mother had to admit it, though that was almost more than she could handle. She and the boy's father had gotten divorced about a year before. The man, it seemed, was very good and caring with the boy, but not with her. Specifically, he visited regularly, but he had fallen way behind in his alimony payments. The woman's lawyer gave her the typical lawyer's solution: no alimony, no visits.

The woman was delighted with that idea. She didn't need the alimony; she was a successful businesswoman. And she was so angry with her ex for going off with another woman that she would do anything to punish him.

So she stopped the father from visiting his son. As soon as the visits stopped, the night terrors started.

Obviously, the two were connected. When I pointed this out to her, she nodded slowly in reluctant agreement. But she argued that the rotten SOB was still supposed to pay her alimony.

That might be true, but I reminded her that to begin with she really didn't need that money. More important, in her effort to punish her former husband, she was damaging her little boy. "He'll be the long-term sufferer," I told her. "Not his father. These night terrors won't simply vanish. Keep his father away from him and he'll keep you awake for at least the next month. He'll grow awfully angry and blame you. 'Why are you keeping Daddy away from me?' he'll want to know."

She left my office and never returned. I did learn from their pediatrician, however, that soon after that the father was allowed to visit again and the night terrors stopped.

The alimony weapon is a terrible one that lawyers

continually recommend to their clients. The lawyers, of course, want to get their clients what they think they are entitled to. I understand that. What they and their clients lose sight of in their anger is the welfare of the child trapped in the middle of the fight. Just when he needs his father the most, that significant man is cut off from him.

Single Mothers, New Lovers

Happily, life goes on. Usually, there is a period of adjustment, some call it mourning, for about a year before the divorced mother becomes a social person again. A number of mothers who reach that point have come to me, concerned about the effect of their dating, of new men, on their children.

I think it's best to apply some caution. If a certain number of different men appear to pick Mother up and meet the children, that doesn't mean much. But it would if a certain number of different men also came home with Mother and shared her bed in a casual way.

If there's sex in the relationship, it's far better and less confusing for the children if it's confined to the man's apartment, with Mother returning home afterward.

If a relationship develops to the point where the woman and her lover want a live-in arrangement, that should be a major commitment for both. The woman should feel secure that this is a man she wants not only as her lover but also as the new male model for her children.

She should try to introduce him naturally to her children and their life. The more they can all do together the better. Maybe they all can spend a number of Sundays together. No man is going to be immediately accepted by children as a replacement for their father. But within the new context, the man should feel reasonably comfortable and able to make a long-term commitment.

SERIOUS ILLNESS AND HOSPITALIZATION

I do a great deal of work with children who are seriously ill and hospitalized. One of the first questions their parents ask me is, ''How much should we tell him?''

In fact, it is important for the child's mental and physical health that parents tell their child as clearly as they can as much as he can understand about what has happened and what's going to happen.

I have seen parents get the sad news from their doctor that their child is going to need surgery—or chemotherapy, or whatever—and go back into their child's room with tears streaming down their face.

''What's wrong, Mommy, what's wrong?'' the poor three-year-old says.

''Nothing's wrong, dear,'' the mother responds. ''Nothing's wrong.''

It's pathetic and almost ludicrous. Obviously, the child sees that something terrible is wrong, and no matter how dreadful a mother might think the news is, the child's fantasies are infinitely worse.

She will imagine that somehow her world, which consists only of her and Mommy and Daddy, is going to end. What else could it be if Mommy and Daddy are both so upset? Maybe she's going to be eaten by a giant frog. Maybe her parents are going away and will never come back, a common fantasy. Or maybe she's going to be given away to the people in the next bed, another common terror.

Not only will you spare your child awful fantasy fears, but you might well improve her chances of surviving by telling her the truth. Our experience is that children told the truth cooperate and work for their own recovery.

I think of a four-year-old whom we sat down—and your doctor should do the explaining with you—and told that she had a tumor on her spine. It could spread and the only way to stop that from happening was for her to take very strong medicine, medicine that might make her sick to her stomach, and it might make her hair fall out as well.

She hates her chemotherapy treatments, but she co-operates with it. She says ouch every time; it hurts, and she yells at her doctor. She has her own little hospital kit and a dollhouse hospital in which she gets to be the doctor, to identify with the aggressor. We break off needles and give her the syringes so she can go around sticking all her pretend patients, who, of course, are doctors.

She has lost hair too. That's distressing for a four-year-old girl, but much less traumatic than waking up one morning, unwarned, and finding her pillow full of her hair.

For cardiac patients, cooperation with the surgical process is essential, and again our experience is that the more we tell them and they understand, the better.

After surgery they have a chest-length incision, but they must cough and clear their lungs or they could get pneumonia, which would complicate and greatly pro-long their recovery. It hurts terribly, even with pain-killers. As part of their preparation, the day before the surgery we have a rehearsal. They go through all the therapeutic things that they are going to do, including blowing whistles and blowing up balloons.

We tell them: "You're going to have to do this, blow on these things, even though it hurts. It's the only way you're going to get well."

They don't fool themselves. They do what they have to do.

In the old days, these same children were told every-thing was going to be just fine, and when it came time to cough they wouldn't do it. It hurt too much.

There was another child who wasn't told that he was going into the hospital for major open-heart surgery. Nobody on our staff knew it, but he had been told he was simply going in for a weekend of tests. After the operation, the child turned into a fetal ball. He wouldn't move, wouldn't talk to anyone or do anything, became mute.

He almost died three times, not because of the heart operation, but because of secretions. The nurses had to wrestle with him to suction clear secretions from his lungs. Because he wouldn't cough, secretions would pile up in his lungs and they wouldn't work. He'd turn blue.

For three years after he left the hospital, that boy was impossible both at home and in school.

So there is no question in our minds of the importance of truthfulness. As I've mentioned elsewhere, at Tisch University Hospital in New York we tell parents that we won't perform any operations or procedures until their child has been told the whole story.

Normally, it's best to have the doctor explain everything along with the parents.

The Right Hospital

One of the major concerns about hospitalization for any child up to the age of six is the fear of separation. And that's true whether he's going in for open-heart surgery or something minor such as a tonsillectomy or a hernia repair.

So find a hospital where you and your child will not be separated, where there are some living-in arrangements for parents.

This does not mean, by the way, that you can't go home, or that one parent can't spell another. But certainly during the crisis of an acute illness, the first few days in the hospital, the parent of greatest attachment to the child—usually the mother—should be around most if not all of the time.

The hospital should also provide the resources a child of this age needs.

A sick, hospitalized child wants to prove to himself

that his body is functional. He does it by being active, playing and doing things.

So to the limits of his condition, he should be able to do that. Even if he's on bed rest, he should have a good supply of toys and people to play with him.

A playroom should be available. Children who can move around are going to be assured that whatever they have is not deadly because they can throw themselves into familiar games and activities.

The hospital should be a welcome place for you and your child. And you should be able to visit it beforehand.

There should be a significant person, like a charge nurse, who can be your special agent, who can lead you through and help you in whatever crisis might arise. It's been estimated that a child coming in for surgery has to deal with fifty new people within his first twenty-four hours, which is a lot to cope with. If you have a central figure like that nurse to help you and your child navigate through everything, it can make a great difference.

Psychological Recovery

After major surgery—or, in the case of cancer, during the lengthy period of treatment—how a child responds psychologically depends very much on how his family responds.

I have seen parents who are so frightened and fearful that they turn their children into infants. They won't let them do anything or go anywhere.

It's a phenomenon we first encountered with adults who had operations for rheumatic heart disease. They would recover and become perfectly normal physiologically, but psychologically they were crippled. They remained afraid. They were in wheelchairs, and years later they were still in wheelchairs and they wouldn't, couldn't, give them up without extensive rehabilitation and therapy.

The same pattern can be found with recovering children and their parents. The children can do marvelously on their own. But in a family where everyone is waiting for the little thing to sneeze, the child will also become fearful.

Some parents compound the anxiety of this situation by projecting their own guilt on it. They imagine that they are responsible for the child's illness, that they took the child into a room somewhere and the defenseless child contracted the disease. Or, with cancer, that it was their bad genes that conveyed the cancer to their child.

One of my former cancer patients actually became anorexic as an adolescent. Every time the slightest thing went wrong, she became anorexic and was rushed to the hospital by her parents. She used to recover rather quickly when separated from her parents. But she couldn't be cured psychologically in such an anxious family constellation. She had to get away from home, live in a boarding school, before she could really improve and stabilize her condition.

To be sure, living with cancer treatment for three to five years can be very difficult. But the objective in cancer rehabilitation is for the patient to maintain as high a level of functioning as her physical condition allows.

What I try to do is get the parent to rise above their own anxiety. Given a chance, extremely ill children can do very well in the right family atmosphere. And the right family atmosphere means an attitude of living life as fully as possible as long as you can. It is hoped that it will be a long life, but if it stops, it stops. It takes a lot of courage on the part of everyone.

Sometimes parents choose denial, which might seem the best way at first, especially with young children. But that won't work over the long term.

I think of one couple who was very bright, but also very frightened. Don't tell our daughter anything, they said to me. They had both lived all their lives under the notion that if you made believe something unpleasant wasn't there, it would go away.

I told them that first of all, if they insisted on that approach they'd have to take their daughter elsewhere for treatment. We wouldn't take care of her, because we were not being allowed to take care of her properly.

Beyond that, their daughter was going to have to undergo extensive chemotherapy treatment for years. How did they possibly expect to hide the reality of it from her? All they'd do would be to destroy their relationship with her.

They understood, and the daughter is doing wonderfully. The mother remains terribly frightened and gets panicky over the slightest problem, so I still treat her. But her anxiety doesn't get in the way of the proper rehabilitation for her daughter.

INDEX

About the Authors

DR. H. PAUL GABRIEL has taught and practiced at New York University Medical Center and Bellevue Hospital Center in New York City for over twenty years. He is currently director of the pediatric psychiatric liaison program at NYU. Dr. Gabriel has served as a consultant to the National Institute of Mental Health and is a fellow of the American Academy of Child Psychiatry.

ROBERT WOOL, author of six books, is in training at the National Psychological Association for Pschoanalysis. He lives with his wife and their two daughters, twelve and nine, in New York City.